GOD'S CALL TO THE
SINGLE ADULT

Michael Cavanaugh

GOD'S CALL TO THE SINGLE ADULT

Michael Cavanaugh

Copyright © 1986 by Michael P. Cavanaugh
Printed in the United States of America
ISBN: 0-88368-187-0

Compiled, arranged, and edited
by Susan M. McCarthy

*Edited and prepared for Whitaker House
by David L. Young*

DEDICATION

It strikes me that any measure of success I have known has come because God has surrounded me with selfless people who have worked for my success above their own. I would like to dedicate this book to these kind, serving people whose names often don't get mentioned.

First of all, to the full-time Mobilized To Serve and B.A.S.I.C. staff, both those who have served in the past—Pam Thompson, Manny Josbena, and Dennis Okoniewski—and those who presently serve—Dave and Cathy Allport, Barb Coyle, Anne Canon, Sue McCarthy, Debra Rogers, Dave Phenes and Tony Martorana. No law could demand their level of commitment and service. It comes from the love of God.

Secondly, to my wife, Terri Marie Cavanaugh, who loves me so much that she gives me courage to keep on doing, and who loves God so much she lets me go when He calls.

CONTENTS

FOREWORD

I was 27 and single when I suddenly became aware that God might be calling me to a life of singleness for Him.

What would that mean to me? I wondered. What would I be missing? What would others think? Would I be looked on as a reject or an opportunity for the church would-be matchmaker? What about temptation? My sexuality? What purpose could my singleness possibly fulfill? Does God really call some to a life of singleness, or is it due to a flaw? Am I a leftover or "second best"?

These and many other questions demanded an answer! And as I wrestled with these quandaries and struggled to come to a place of resolve in those younger days, I longed for someone to speak to the subject.

Today, someone has—Mike Cavanaugh! In this book Mike cuts to the heart of the issue and presents scriptural answers. From a wealth of experience in counseling, ministering with and the leading of singles, come real life answers.

While reading this manuscript, I began to walk through my own history as a single starting a missionary organization. As I came to rest in God's will, He led me to meet and marry Darlene, a nurse who, by choice, had a career and fulfillment as a single.

As I read, I also pondered some of those I have met who have influenced my life and were called to singleness: Corrie Ten Boom, Bill Gothard, Basilea Schlink, Harley Vale, Mother Teresa, and others. How did I perceive them? Not as less than normal! And certainly not as leftovers. They were people of destiny!

You, too, are a person of incredible potential and destiny. Although this book relates to your singleness, you will discover singleness is neither the problem nor even the true issue! Destiny—God's and your's—fulfillment—God's and your's—is the issue. That's what this book and your life are all about.

Loren Cunningham

(Loren Cunningham is the President of Youth With A Mission International.)

Chapter Introduction

YOU ARE NOT HALF A COOKIE

Have you ever had the feeling that you were less than a person? Somehow, as Jane married Joe, Denise married Mark, and Pam married Jim, you began to feel like a leftover in life or the last person picked for a baseball team.

You remember how it was in school. Two kids stood in front of a group of their peers and, one by one, began picking people for their team. Slowly the crowd began to get smaller and smaller, until "the crowd" became a group, and "the group" became a few.

You watched nervously as the group dwindled. Inside, you shouted, "Pick me! Oh, pick me! Oh, *please* pick me." You didn't want to be the last person picked—the one the other guy took because he had to.

Finally, the dreaded moment came. There you stood with another unathletic-looking person. Neither of you were prime picks. But if you could be the last person *chosen*—there was a fifty-fifty chance now, the best odds yet—then at least you would retain a little self-respect.

The choice was made. It wasn't you. The other person heaved a big sigh of relief, while you lowered your shoulders, bowed your head, and slunk over to the team that *had to take you*. You didn't even want to look at them. You could just imagine how everyone was taking this. It was like getting Charlie Brown. You were the death blow to the team—a leftover.

Many singles feel that way about their singleness. They feel rejected, hurt, and inferior. There's got to be something wrong with me, they think. Look at Jane. Look at Terri. Look at Tom. They all have somebody. What's wrong with me? I'm still single.

Sometimes, family and friends reinforce these negative feelings. They try to pair singles off or infer they're somehow less than other adults, simply because they aren't married. "When are you going to settle down?" parents moan, as though the only balanced, rooted lifestyle could be found in marriage.

Many churches and para-church ministries take a similar position. They embrace the widely held opinion that ultimate fulfillment comes through marriage and end up selling singles short in the process.

When I began thinking about ministering to single adults, I did a lot of research on what was done for them already. What I found out disturbed me. Many churches and ministries missed the mark in coping with what they called "the single adult problem."

Almost consistently, they saw themselves either as social directors or psychiatrists. They concentrated all their efforts on providing recreational activities for "the unmated" or offering teachings and discussion groups centered on helping "poor, maladjusted, lonely" single people with their problems. Singleness was treated as a deadly disease, curable only by matrimony.

I received a call once from an elder of a local church,

whose conversation revealed he felt this way. "Look," he told me, "I have a woman in my church, a former missionary, and, well, I know you meet a lot of singles in your ministry. Maybe you've met someone that she might get along with." He was doing what he thought was right. I understood that. But I also knew that, by his actions, he was telling her she wasn't a full person just because she wasn't married.

"All you're feeding her with that kind of thinking," I told him, "is the same kind of feeling she already has about herself: she's a useless nobody unless somebody comes along and carries her off."

I've heard thinking like that called Knight in Shining Armor Syndrome. It says a person is not complete until someone on horseback comes riding over the mountain, sweeps them off their feet, and carries them off to the Land of Wholeness.

Many singles have a Knight in Shining Armor Syndrome. They walk around feeling as though they are only half a person, almost visualizing themselves with half a body or half a brain—until they find the other half that will make them complete.

They feel like half an Oreo cookie—the one *without* the cream—in search of their other half. Without the other half, they believe they're, at best, a crumbly chocolate wafer of no distinction—definitely not an Oreo, in any case.

This feeling of inadequacy feeds yet a second assumption—that all their problems stem from singleness. "If I'm lonely, it's because I'm single. If I lack purpose or direction, it's because I'm single. If I'm emotionally unstable, it's because I'm single. If I'm sexually frustrated and unfulfilled, it's because I'm single."

Faced with these feelings and the negative counsel of family, friends, and church alike, all singles want to do is escape. So they fall into a hard, driving search to find Mr. or Miss Right. They bend, twist, manipulate, and run to this function or that rally—all in an effort to bring their "curse" of singleness to an end.

But, after a while, the search becomes a snare. Single adults who get caught in the "gotta get a guy/gotta get a girl" syndrome wake up one morning to find themselves living in limbo. They're afraid to make a move for fear that it might keep them from meeting that mythical someone.

Consequently, they make no permanent plans, set no permanent goals, and hesitate to make any life-changing decisions because they're still waiting for "the right person" to come along.

I knew one single guy, a very prosperous man, who was caught in that kind of trap. He had a good job, made excellent money, and lived in a beautiful, modern apartment complex.

One day, I went to visit him at his home and was amazed at what I saw. This affluent and successful man's place was still furnished with old, hand-me-down furniture—Salvation Army, Early Crate. I asked him why he hadn't bought new things. Money wasn't a problem. "I thought about doing that once," he said, "but, well, what if the future Miss Right doesn't like the furniture I buy?"

This man was living his life in a holding pattern, afraid to make any move until his lifetime partner came along. When she did, he thought, she would give him a vision for his life. She would fit him into the mold designed for him. She would set him on the "right track.'' Then he could get on with living.

But by living like this, he was actually holding himself back from experiencing the joy and fulfillment he so earnestly sought. By rejecting his singleness and longing after the supposedly greener grass of married life, he was missing out on the great things God wanted to do with him and through him in this hour. Thus he felt empty, lonely, and purposeless.

Many single people struggle with the same issues and the same feelings. They, too, live in a kind of twilight zone, waiting for Mr. or Miss Right to rescue them from their plight. They, too, look to marriage as some kind of fairyland where all their dreams will come true. They, too, believe their singleness is some kind of curse on their life, signifying their own lack of worth and ability to contribute in any substantial way to those around them. And, like the man I just told you about, they, too, are robbed daily of the very things they seek—fulfillment, happiness, and joy.

God doesn't see your singleness as a curse. Neither does He see you as a worthless nobody, ready for the junk pile. To Him, you are a person of promise, ability, talent, and skill, who, formed and empowered by Him, can accomplish great things for His Kingdom. To Him, your season of singleness provides a rare opportunity for you to grow in relationship with Him and serve Him one hundred percent, without distraction. It is a time for knowing and serving Him in a way that is uniquely possible to singles alone.

I believe God would like you to know six things about your singleness—six Biblical understandings of this special season of your life—that will enable you to embrace this new fellowship with your Lord and help you to be all you can be for Him—right now. Come with me. Let's explore.

Chapter One

COMPLETE IN CHRIST

You are a complete person apart from any romantic relationship you will ever have.

That's right. The person you are today, with all your abilities and talents, callings and desires, is a full person in the Kingdom of God. You are capable of doing great things for Him—not sometime down the road, but *right now*—in the town where you live, in the church you attend, and among the people whose lives you touch.

No romantic relationship, however permanent, will ever make you more satisfied, more complete, or more ready to serve Christ than you are today. You are a complete, whole person that God is interested in using now for Kingdom purposes.

"But that can't be. I certainly don't *feel* like a whole person," you may say. "My life is in shambles. I'm lonely. I'm sexually frustrated. I'm confused. I feel unsettled and directionless. Surely if I were married, everything would be better. I wouldn't be lonely any more. I wouldn't have any more struggles with my sex drive. I'd feel whole, and I'd have a real purpose for my life."

But that's simply not true. If you haven't dealt with the cause of your loneliness before you get married, it isn't going to evaporate after you say "I do." If you haven't found purity in your struggles with sexuality as a single person, marriage isn't going to make you pure. If you don't feel complete as a single person, just being married to another person isn't going to give you an immediate sense of wholeness or purpose, either.

Why? Because the problems you're dealing with aren't caused by your singleness. Just one look at some of the marriages around you will give you evidence that what I'm saying is true.

Some of the loneliest people I know are *married* people. They're married, yes, but in every real way they are very much alone. Each night they lie in bed next to someone with whom they cannot communicate. In that utter darkness, with tears streaming down their cheeks, they experience the worst kind of loneliness any person can know. Sydney Harris said it quite well:

> Real loneliness consists not in being alone,
> but in being with the wrong person in the
> suffocating darkness of a room in which no
> deep communication is possible.

How true and how pervasive that is. Loneliness is obviously not a product of singleness. In fact, it's not confined to singles in any way. You see, whether a person is married or single, only a wholehearted relationship with Christ can meet the emotional and spiritual needs that lead to loneliness.

Forbidden Attractions

Sexual temptation will not be quenched just by getting married either. Take a look at the facts. In almost any newspaper, you can find listings for pornographic movies. On city streets, you'll find people selling their own flesh. On any number of magazine racks, you'll see X-rated material available for purchase.

Do you think only single people watch those movies? Do you think only singles read *Playboy*? Do you think only singles get involved with prostitutes?

What about all the sexual crimes you read about in the newspaper? Do you think only single people commit them? What about the struggle with promiscuity or masturbation? Do you think only single people have these problems?

Of course not. Just as many married people struggle with sexual problems, go to pornographic movies, visit with prostitutes, and read perverted magazines as single people. Being married doesn't instantly solve the problem.

Why? Because what attracts people to these sinful pleasures is not the sin itself but the idea that it is stolen. *They enjoy the forbidden*.

In Proverbs 9:17, "the woman Folly" says:

> Stolen water is sweet; And bread eaten
> in secret is pleasant.

Have you developed a taste for stolen water? Does the idea of taking something forbidden attract you?

Take a look at the sexual sin you're struggling with now. Something about it lures you. Is it just the pleasure of the act, or is the pleasure somehow rooted in the forbidden? I believe, if you'll look closely enough, you'll discover the latter is true. Sex has taken on an outer coating of the forbidden. While you're involved in it, your spirit man is very aware that it's wrong. But you've developed such a taste for the forbidden that you can't seem to resist it. It draws you in, pulls you under, and devours you.

Many people think that once they get married their desire for the forbidden will go away. They believe their struggles against sexual sin should end because they can now have sex righteously within marriage. But that's not what happens. Because the righteous relationship of marriage does not satisfy the person's taste for the forbidden, they're left struggling with the same old temptations as before. They lust after the forbidden. It's the forbidden they really want.

That's why your struggles with sexual sin aren't going to go away the minute you get married. That's why you'll still be tempted and fall prey to the lure of pornography—movies, magazines, and books—and illicit sex. That's why you'll struggle with unfaithfulness, even though you really love your spouse. You've got a taste for stolen water. If this desire is not dealt with before marriage, it may end up ruining an otherwise promising relationship.

If you have a desire for the forbidden, you have to deal with that desire *now.* You have to lay it at the feet of Jesus and let it die. Let it die now, so you may live.

"But, Mike, how is that possible? I mean, I *really* struggle with this problem. All I need to do is start thinking about something, and pretty soon I'm doing it. I don't want to do it, but somehow I end up doing it anyway."

But that's your first mistake. You *think* about it. You allow that sinful thought to run through your brain over and over again until, finally, it causes you to sin. That's right—*causes* you to sin. You see, the thought itself isn't a sin. That's temptation. It only becomes sin when you do something about it.

Many people don't know that, though. A wrong thought comes into their head, and they immediately think they've fallen. "How could a Christian think like that? That's so sinful," they think. Then they just give in.

Listen. You've got to recognize something here: In this life, you're going to be tempted. Every day wrong thoughts are going to float through your mind. The problem comes when you nurse those tempting thoughts and let them germinate in your heart until they cause you to sin.

Take the example of Eve and the serpent. The serpent tempted Eve, but it was she who allowed it to fester in her heart and, finally, cause her to sin. Let's read the account from Genesis 3:1-6:

> Now the serpent was more crafty than any beast of the field which the Lord God had made. And he said to the woman, "Indeed, has God said, 'You shall not eat from any tree of the garden'?" And the woman said to the serpent, "From the fruit of the trees of the garden we may eat; but from the fruit of the tree which is in the middle of the garden, God has said, 'You shall not eat from it or touch it, lest you die.'"

19

And the serpent said to the woman, "You surely shall not die! For God knows that in the day you eat from it your eyes will be opened, and you will be like God, knowing good and evil." When the woman saw that the tree was good for food, and that it was a delight to the eyes, and that the tree was desirable to make one wise, she took from its fruit and ate.

There they were, the fatal words of temptation: "For God knows that in the day you eat from it your eyes will be opened, and you will be like God, knowing good and evil." What a lure! It prompted Eve to have bad thoughts about the Lord and to lust for godhood.

But Eve hadn't done anything wrong yet. These were just thoughts, transmitted to her from the adversary. The problem came when she allowed herself to meditate on those thoughts and to consider, for herself, whether or not to eat the fruit of that tree. By allowing herself to be seduced by those thoughts rather than allowing God's command to do battle against temptation, she fell into sin.

In the same way, Satan will tempt you today. He will drop ungodly thoughts into your mind—"Go ahead. See that movie. Who will know? Go ahead. Take a look at that magazine. What harm could it do? Go ahead. Give in to that sexual desire. You're only human." That will happen. In this life, it's guaranteed. But it's what you *do* with those thoughts that will determine the outcome.

When the first seed of a thought of sexual sin comes into your heart, don't allow it to take a foothold. Don't sit there contemplating the idea. Don't even meditate on how wrong it is to be thinking that way. Just come back at that thought, full force, with the Word of God. That's what Jesus did when Satan tempted Him. Matthew 4:1-11 says,

> Then Jesus was led up by the Spirit into the wilderness to be tempted by the devil. And after He fasted forty days and forty nights, He then became hungry. And the tempter came and said to Him, "If You are the Son of God, command that these stones become bread." But He answered and said, "It is written, 'Man shall not live on bread alone, but on every word that proceeds out of the mouth of God.'"
>
> Then the devil took Him into the holy city; and he had Him stand on the pinnacle of the temple, and said to Him, "If You are the Son of God throw Yourself down; for it is written, 'He will give His angels charge concerning You;' and 'In their hands they will bear You up, lest You strike Your foot against a stone.'" Jesus said to him, "On the other hand, it is written 'You shall not put the Lord your God to the test.'"
>
> Again, the devil took Him to a very high mountain, and showed Him all the kingdoms of the world, and their glory; and he said to Him, "All these things will I give You, if You fall down and worship me." Then Jesus said to him, "Be gone, Satan." For it is written, 'You shall worship the Lord

your God and serve Him only.'''

Then the devil left Him; and behold, angels came and began to minister to Him.

The temptations in this passage were real for Jesus. First of all, after forty days and forty nights, you can be sure He was very hungry.

Secondly, since His trust in His Father was so faultless and complete, you can be sure He was tempted to step out on that word of protection from Psalm 91.

Thirdly, who more than Jesus wanted to ransom the world and bring it back into fellowship with the Father? It was His purpose in coming. Surely, this was His deepest desire. Yet, to succumb to any one of these temptations meant to submit to Satan and fall into sin.

How did Jesus do battle? He used the Word of God. He brought the Word to bear against the area of temptation—time after time after time—until the devil was defeated.

You need to do the same thing. Memorize some Scripture verses pertaining to your area of weakness—ones that show God's strength on your behalf and counteract the thoughts of the enemy. Then, every time an ungodly thought comes into your mind, come against it with those verses. There will be a struggle. There was for Christ Himself. But remember, greater is He that is in you than He that is in the world. (See 1 John 4:4.) You will have victory. . .in Jesus, by the Word.

One Plus One Equals One

Another thing that needs to be tackled and tossed

out of your life as a Christian single person is this myth: marriage will make you complete.

No way. Marriage will not make you complete. There isn't a person in the whole world who can do that for you. If you feel like half a person now as a single, you won't feel any different just because you get married. As a matter of fact, if you get married while you're still feeling like half a person, you'll try to draw your sense of wholeness from your partner, and that puts an impossible strain on any relationship.

No human relationship—no matter how intimate, no matter how vital, no matter how enriching—can provide ultimate fulfillment for you. Ultimate fulfillment comes from a deeper relationship with Jesus Christ.

"Now wait," you may say. "Doesn't God say in His Word that 'the two shall become one?' Doesn't that mean that one-half plus one-half equals one? Doesn't that mean God wants to complete me with another person?"

No. I don't believe that's what God is saying here at all. Where would the miracle be in God bringing two half-people together and making them one person? Besides, in romantic relationships, one-half plus one-half does *not* equal one whole. If you bring two half-people together, all you'll get is two insecure, dependent people struggling to draw from one another what they should only be getting from the Lord. That's a sad situation, and many bad marriages have been built on that shaky ground.

The real miracle disclosed in this verse is that God takes two whole, distinct, fulfilled individuals—blessed with their own unique talents and abilities—and makes them one new person together. Now *that's* a miracle.

But God doesn't advocate that you look for someone to complete you. He says, "Look to Me as your completion, and the rest will follow." Paul says in 1 Corinthians 7:24,27 (Amplified Version),

> So, brethren, in whatever station or state or condition of life each one was when he was called, let him continue there, with and close to God. . . . Are you bound to a wife? Do not seek to be free. Are you free from a wife? Do not seek a wife.

God is calling you to be content in Him first. He is calling you to look to Him in your loneliness, in your sexual struggles, and in your feelings of rejection and hurt. He is calling you to be complete in Him.

"But, Mike, doesn't Proverbs say somewhere that 'He who finds a wife, finds a good thing'?"

Yes. That's Proverbs 18:22.

"Well, how am I supposed to find a wife (or husband) if I don't look for one?"

Good point. At least on the surface. This verse does seem to indicate the value of searching for a mate, doesn't it? There's just one problem, though. That word "find" in the Hebrew doesn't mean "to find by searching for." It means "to discover along the way." This verse is saying, "If you're wrapped up with the Lord, submitting to Him and serving Him according to His will, and along comes someone who ends up being your mate, that's a good thing."

"But what if I do that, then God leaves me single? What if I allow myself to be happy and fulfilled as a single person? Won't God look down and say, 'Oh, so he's *happy* being single. Well, I'll leave him that way'?''

That's the risk many singles feel they're taking. They're petrified of being truly happy singles because they think God will look down, see they're happy, and believe they don't need to get married.

Because of this fear they drag themselves around, day by day, refusing to get anything out of their single life. And all the while, they're looking up to God, saying, "See, God? See? I'm miserable. See? I'm one of those who really *needs* to be married. I really *need* that thing in my life. Please." And they use all their energy to make themselves miserable rather than taking their time as a single person and using it for the glory of God.

But if you use your singleness just as a waiting period for Mr. or Miss Right, you're not really getting the most out of life as God intended. You're allowing yourself to live in a twilight zone, a no man's land without vision, purpose, or meaning. And a person without purpose, vision, or meaning is bound to be discouraged, defeated, and depressed. They're bound to feel worthless. They're bound to live in a world of past rejections and failures. They're bound to feel lifeless and unfulfilled.

Why? Because they are. They've allowed themselves to be caught in limbo, waiting for Mr. or Miss Right, rather than using their singleness to glorify God.

Let me tell you something: it's in giving your life in service to God and others that the fulfillment, the purpose, and the joy you seek will come to you. Only when you're willing to give yourself one hundred percent to the Lord will you truly begin to live. And only when you're willing to submit to the Lord in this wholehearted way will you achieve the kind of balance that can bring the mate of God's own choosing into your life.

Pushing The Panic Button

Some single people do give themselves in whole-hearted service to the Lord. They lay their desire for marriage upon the altar before God and start serving Him one hundred percent.

Then, one day, a particular birthday rolls around. They reach 25, 30, 35—whatever age they thought they should be married—and find themselves still single.

Immediately, they push the panic button. "Oh, no. Oh, no. I'm not married. I'm going to end up old and lonely. I'm never going to have kids. I'm never going to have the kind of relationship I always wanted. The pickings are getting slim now, too. Soon I'll be too old." And they launch into a frantic search for a partner. They don't care what the person looks like, how they feel about anything, or what they do for a living. They don't have to be Mr. or Miss Right anymore. Any *marginally acceptable* person will do.

A woman at one of the singles conferences my ministry conducts said that people in her church call that the "Bride of Frankenstein Syndrome." You know the story. It involves a scientist who pumps bolts of electricity into dead bodies in an attempt to bring them back to life.

In the same way, she said, single people who have "Bride of Frankenstein Syndrome" drag unlikely, spiritually dead people into church, present them to their pastor, and say, "Pastor, pump some life into this person, please!''

But when you do something like this—dig around in the dirt for somebody, anybody to marry you—you never know what you'll come up with. And chances are good you'll end up married to someone who doesn't share your vision for service.

I've known people like this. They wanted to be married more than anything else in the world. So they made that their first priority in life. Oh, they wanted to serve the Lord, but, like so many other singles, they felt they needed to get married first. ''God, I want to serve you. But let me get married first. Then we'll take care of the rest of it.'' So they accomplished their goal: they found someone and got married. But then, too late, they realized their partner didn't share the same vision for service that they did. Their mate became a weight, holding them back from the things God wanted to do with their life, rather than the catalyst they hoped their mate would be for service.

By putting marriage ahead of God's design for their life, they ended up married to someone who didn't fit into God's plan for them.

Now, God can use a relationship like that. He will, as the Bible says, cause all things to work together for good. (See Romans 8:28.) But that person should have waited, allowed himself to be led by God, and moved into the service He had prepared for him. Then marriage, if it were to come along, would have grown out of that service and been in keeping with God's perfect will for the person's life. Also, it would have allowed him to be used by God as a single person rather than causing him to fritter away months and months of time pursuing someone—anyone—to marry him.

So, it's important, on several levels, to realize that you are a complete person *right now* in the Kingdom of God.

It's important because, in knowing this, you'll be able to begin serving Christ—right now—in your church and your community.

It's important because it will give you a right understanding of marriage—not as a cure-all for what ails you but as a calling of God and a miracle of life, drawing two complete people together as one new person and joining them in common service to the Lord.

It's important because it will cause you to recognize the true source of healing, completion, and fulfillment in your life—the Lord Jesus Christ.

Knowing these three things will help you keep balance—in your relationship with God, in your Christian walk, and in your relationship with others and yourself.

I remember the time God taught me these principles. While in Bible school, I was dating a lovely girl. Everything seemed perfect between us. She was a Christian, and so was I. We both loved the Lord and seemed very much in love with each other.

I dreamt about this girl all the time. I imagined the home we would have together. . .the white picket fence, the flowers in the yard, and the children. My dreams filled up all my time when we were apart, and I thought a lot about the day I would finally ask her to marry me.

Then one day, out of the blue, just before school recessed for the summer, she told me we were through. Just like that. No explanations.

I tried to talk to her to find out what went wrong,

but I couldn't make any headway. Then school closed, and we went home.

It was hard going into the summer like that. I couldn't stop thinking about her, and I couldn't stop crying. I grieved day and night. Sometimes I would stare at the silent phone for hours. A few times I even picked up the receiver, dialed the first few digits of her number, and hung up.

Everything seemed to remind me of her, of us, and of what I had lost. Even on my way home from church on Sundays, she was in my thoughts. I would look at the happy families and feel the pain of knowing it could never be so with us. The emptiness in the seat next to mine was as big as the empty feeling in my heart. I was devastated.

At the time I was ministering in a church a few miles from home. As I drove back from services each Sunday, I passed an ice cream stand. Usually a few pretty girls stood outside talking and eating. Even though I was sure most of them weren't Christians, my loneliness made me long to get to know them.

For several weeks I didn't do much besides stare as I drove by. I thought about stopping and even rehearsed some of the lines I would say. But I never got up the courage to do anything.

Then one Sunday I finally became determined. "This time," I thought, "I feel really ready to talk to someone." So I buzzed into the parking lot with my little Volkswagen—VW's were really "in" back then—pushed open the door, and strolled casually up to the counter. Strategically, I placed myself a few feet from one of the cutest girls in the place. I was all ready to make my approach.

Suddenly, behind me, I heard a high, thin voice calling my name. Turning around, I saw a little old lady from the church running over to say hello. I was mortified. What if this woman had seen me. . . *in action* ?

I wish I could say that ended my attempts at the ice cream stand, but it didn't. I tried the same thing a couple more times, but each time I ran into somebody I knew. Finally, I resigned myself to a summer. . .alone. . .with *the Lord*.

As God would have it, I got an apartment that summer next door to a Christian couple. The woman and I became friends.

Since this woman was married, there was no question in my mind about ever dating her. She was just a nice Christian woman to fellowship with.

This meant I had to learn to relate to her as a human being. That was a new idea for me. For as long as I could remember, there had only been two ways to relate to women: the first, as my mother; the second, as my date. But this was different than either of those. This was my sister in the Lord.

As the summer progressed and our friendship developed, the Lord revealed to me a rich relationship that I had never experienced. It was deep, and it was warm. But it lacked the tension I had felt in dating relationships. I was free to enjoy this person for herself alone, not for some role I was hoping she would play later on.

That same summer I came upon a book by a monk named Thomas a Kempis. It was entitled, *Imitation Of Christ*. When I saw who it was written by, I thought, "Oh, this is for me. A monk." (I was really engrossed in living alone and chaste for God that summer.)

That book was the clincher for everything God had been teaching me through my friendship with that married woman.

One section remains as fresh in my mind today as it did the first time I read it. It said,

> Whoever intends to come to an inward fixing of his heart upon God and to have the grace of devotion must, with our Savior, Christ, withdraw from the world. No man can safely mingle among people, save he would gladly be solitary if he could. No man is secure in a high position save he would gladly be a follower. No man can firmly command, save he has gladly learned to obey.

I can still remember how those words hit home. Every word seemed packed with meaning. The sentences stood out as clearly as if someone had outlined them with a yellow highlighter.

I read them one more time, and the Lord began to speak to me: "Mike, until you're free in your heart to be alone, until you're free in your spirit to relate to women just as women, as though you would never marry them, you'll warp your relationships with them."

Suddenly, my mind was flooded with memories of all the girls I had ever dated, and I realized that every one of my relationships with them had been warped. They had been bent out of shape and destroyed by a driving need inside of me to couple off, to marry, to find "her."

I really believed that finding that "certain someone" would make me complete. I believed that all my needs would be met in her. I believed she would make me feel worthwhile and give me purpose and direction. "With her at my side," I thought, "I could really begin to *live*."

But in striving, stretching, and bending to establish those relationships, I had actually ruined them. I couldn't let my relationships be what they were. My girlfriends couldn't be who they were, and I couldn't be who I was. My identity was so wrapped up in theirs that I worried constantly about losing them. I had no personal sense of identity.

But over that summer God was reshaping my life and redirecting my thoughts. He was taking my eyes off marriage and fixing them instead on Him. He was teaching me that no romantic relationship, no matter how fulfilling and satisfying, could ever give me the completion, the identity, or the purpose I so hungered for. The only person who could give me that was Jesus Christ.

The Source Of Fulfillment

Have you ever yearned for someone so deeply that you've cried yourself to sleep? Have you ever felt completely worthless because you haven't had someone to "go with" like everybody else? Have you ever clung ferociously to a relationship, as if it were your very life support?

Well, God is saying to you today what He said to me in Bible school. No romantic relationship can bring you the fulfillment you seek. True fulfillment comes through a deepening relationship with Jesus Christ.

How can you know that kind of fulfillment in your relationship with Jesus? How can you discover what it really means to be complete in Christ? You can begin by seeing Him as your supplier and giving Him first place in your heart. Only when Jesus is first in your life—before your possessions, before your job, before your career, before every relationship, and before marriage—will you truly be fulfilled.

One single person who grappled with this issue was the rich young ruler:

> And behold, one came to Him and said, "Teacher, what good thing shall I do that I may obtain eternal life?" And He said to him, "Why are you asking Me about what is good? There is only One who is good; but if you wish to enter into life, keep the commandments." He said to Him, "Which ones?" And Jesus said, "You shall not commit murder; you shall not commit adultery; you shall not steal; you shall not bear false Witness; honor your father and mother; and you shall love your neighbor as yourself."
>
> The young man said to Him, "All these things I have kept; what am I still lacking?" Jesus said to him, "If you wish to be complete, go and sell your possessions and give to the poor, and you shall have treasure in heaven; and come, follow Me." But when the young man heard this statement, he went away grieved; for he was one who owned much property (Matthew 19:16-22).

From childhood the rich young ruler had observed the Mosaic Law, obeying every jot and tittle. He never murdered anyone or committed adultery. He never lied, cheated, or stole. He always honored his parents and loved his neighbor as himself. I'm telling you, this was one incredible person. I don't think too many people today—born-again, Spirit-filled believers included—could claim as great a record as he did before God.

Even though he had done all those things, he felt empty and incomplete inside. He was still unfulfilled. So he came to Jesus and asked, "What am I lacking?"

Jesus looked upon the heart of that young gentleman and knew immediately what the problem was. He loved his possessions more than God. So Jesus said to him, "If you wish to be complete, go and sell your possessions and give to the poor, and you shall have treasure in heaven; and come, follow Me."

But the price was too high for this young man. His possessions meant too much to him, and he went away grieved.

How about you? Where is Jesus in your life? Does He truly have first place in your heart? Or is there something else you love too much to surrender to Him?

If there is something inside yourself that you would be unwilling to relinquish in order to obey and follow God, you need to deal with that thing *right now.* You need to come before the Lord and ask Him to enable you to give that thing to Him. Whatever it is—be it your desire for marriage, your material possessions, the comfortable home you live in, the church you've become accustomed to, or the job you love—let go of *that thing.* Pour it out before the Lord, and let Him take first place in your heart. Only when you are willing to surrender your dearest possessions to God will you be able to know completion in Jesus Christ.

Jesus wants to be your fulfillment. He wants to be your consolation in time of loneliness. He wants to be your healer when rejection and hurt cause you pain. He wants to be your victor in areas of sexual struggle. He wants to be your completion in areas of personal fulfillment. He wants to be your strength, causing you to reach out in boldness on behalf of the Gospel and Gospel principles in your daily life. But you need to be willing to let Him be all those things for you.

Let Jesus be your fulfillment. Let Him deal with your loneliness and your battle with sexual sin. Let Him give you a purpose and a vision. Let Him use you—a complete person, full of ability, talent, and skill—now for Kingdom purposes.

If you're willing—and God is willing to make you willing—He promises you fulfillment beyond your wildest dreams. Matthew 6:33 says, ''But seek first His kingdom and His righteousness; and all these things shall be added to you.''

Allow yourself to find fulfillment in Christ. Put Him first in your life. Let Him take care of everything else. He promises He will. And God doesn't lie.

Chapter Two

GOD'S ULTIMATE WILL

Marriage is not God's ultimate will for your life.
"What are you talking about, Michael Cavanaugh?
What do you mean by that? Are you telling me I may
never get married? Are you saying I may be single
forever?" No, I'm not saying that at all.

God is concerned with your marital status. He's concerned with your needs, your desires, and your happiness. He's also concerned with the job that you take,
the place that you live, and the people you live with.
But none of these are His ultimate will for your life.
None of them constitute His final goal for you. None
of them are the ultimate thing He's shooting for.

God's ultimate will for your life is this: to conform
you to the image of His Son. (See Romans 8:29.)

God's not as concerned with location, education, or
any other material thing as He is in making you more
like Jesus. To God, it's not a question of singleness or
marriage, of secular or Christian employment, of living on Main Street, U.S.A. or in Nairobi, Kenya—it's a
question of forming you into the image of His Son.

Your heavenly Father is interested in having you
understand that. He wants you to know that His main

purpose is to make you more like Jesus. And whatever it takes to make you more like His Son, God is willing to do, because everyone in the world needs a reflection of Christ in their life.

That means if God believes the rigors of single living will make you more like Christ, He's going to have you be single, for however long or short a season He believes is necessary. If He feels the married life—with its own set of challenges, pitfalls, and refinements—will cause you to be more like Christ, then He will bring you into that kind of relationship. The bottom line for God is always the same: He wants to make you into an image of His Son because the world needs people who will be mirrors of God, shining the love, the Word, and the good news of Christ into their hearts. He needs Christians—little Christs.

But whatever He chooses, the question for you becomes, "Which do you want more: to be married or to be like Jesus?" Are you allowing God to use your singleness to make you more like Jesus, or is all your energy going into trying to escape the very situation in which God has placed you?

That is the challenge God is facing you with today. That is the question you must answer. That is the issue you must resolve. Who will be Lord of your life? Will it be marriage or Jesus Christ? Which do you love more?

God is calling you to choose His Son. He's calling you to lay down your life for Him, right to marriage and all. God wants you to love Him more than any other thing in your life, and He's calling you to submit to the shaping force of His Spirit, to embrace your singleness and use it, for however long it lasts, for His glory.

Many singles, however, battle against the dealings of God in their life. They see the pain of never having married, of being widowed or divorced as some horrible curse placed upon them, limiting them from truly living a full and happy life. "If only she hadn't walked out on me. If only I were married. If only that relationship had lasted. If only my spouse hadn't died on me. Then I'd be a stronger person in God." They see their experiences as obstacles, when they really should be seeing them as stepping stones, purifying agents designed to strengthen them and make them more like Jesus.

Perhaps you're a single parent. It's not an easy thing to raise children by yourself. But, if you will allow Him to, God wants to use the stress and stretching of single parenting to make you more like Jesus.

Perhaps you're divorced, with no children. Being alone after such a painful experience is a big adjustment. You've got a lot of difficult emotions to deal with, and many times, as a Christian, you can't find other Christians who know how to respond to your situation. I make no attempt to justify their behavior. We in the Church have a long way to go in learning how to minister to the divorced. But neither do I advocate you to take a "poor me" stance that closes you off from allowing God to use this experience to make you more like Him.

In Jesus Christ you have a Friend, Scripture says, that will stick closer than a brother. In Jesus Christ you have One, Isaiah 53 says, that is "acquainted with grief." In Jesus Christ you have One who has experienced rejection and betrayal by those He loved. In Jesus Christ you have the healing and power to overcome the pain and be shaped by your life today into a stronger and clearer reflection of Him.

If you've never been married, the same applies to you. Jesus Himself was an always-single adult. So was Paul from all indication. Isaac, too, was single into his forties. But singleness never prevented them from being used by God. In fact, Paul recommended the single life as one that helped him be closer to the Lord.

God wants to use your singleness to bring you closer to Him. He wants you to begin to come to Him with every need you have. When you're lonely, when you're depressed, when you're experiencing temptation, or when you're looking for purpose and meaning in your life, He wants your first response to be seeking Him.

If you're widowed, God wants to make your widowhood more than a time to mourn the passing of a mate—more than a time to while away the hours. He wants it to be a time of growth and service in Him. If you will let Him, He will use the rigors of widowhood to do just that and to conform you, day by day, into a clearer reflection of His Son.

Whatever type of single person you are, your decision remains the same. You can look at all the things that are happening in your life as problems to be gotten rid of or escaped. Or you can see them as God does—a refiner's fire, meant to strengthen and purify you, step by step, into the image of His Son.

When you choose Jesus, you choose life. When you choose Jesus, you choose freedom. When you choose Jesus, the author and finisher of your faith, and follow after Him, conforming yourself to His image, you don't need to get worked up about geography, location, education, or position any more. At that point, wherever He puts you down will be a good place because you're going to be growing in Him. You're going to be formed into the image of God's Son.

How does God refine you into the image of His Son? By allowing the heat of circumstance to come to bear upon your life.

In both the Old and New Testaments, we see God reflected as a refiner and a purifier. Take, for example, Proverbs 17:3:

> The refining pot is for silver and the furnace for gold, But the Lord tests hearts.

Do you find yourself reading that verse, shaking your head, and thinking, ''Now what does that mean, 'the Lord tests hearts'? Is God going to test me to see if I'll be bad or good?'' No. To be honest, God knows what you're made of. He knows that it's quite likely you would fail. He knows your every weakness and doesn't have to put you to a test to discover them.

The testing referred to in this passage is the kind gold goes through to make it pure. In its raw form, gold has a lot of impurities running through it that mar it. So, in order to get them out and make the gold as fine and pure as possible, it is put into a crucible and heated with intense fire. Under those conditions, the gold liquifies, and the impurities within it rise to the top, appearing as tiny flecks on the gold's surface. A worker then takes a fan or bellows and blows the flecks off the gold's surface.

As more heat is applied, still more flecks surface and again are blown to the side. Finally, the worker takes a scoop and removes whatever impurites are left. In the end, the surface of the metal is mirror-like in purity, and the refiner's face is perfectly reflected.

In the same way, God uses the heat of circumstance to purify you. He lets the stresses and strains of single living touch you so the impurities in your life can rise to the surface and be blown away by the Holy Spirit. Then you will more perfectly reflect the image of His Son to the world.

Trial By Fire

A few years ago, I bought a new car—not a "new" used car but a totally new, "never-owned-by-anyone-but-the-bank-and-me" car.

I was proud of that car. I thought I'd never own one that still had that new smell to it. I grew up in a poor home, and my mom didn't even own a car. We went everywhere by public transport or by foot. So the day I bought my brand new car, I was bursting inside with excitement.

Well, one weekend after we brought the car home, I was outside our apartment putting a new, customized stereo tape deck in the dash. As I was crouched along the front seat working away, I heard my little son, then three years old, come tearing across the graveled lot to greet me. In one of his hands was a fistful of little stones.

As he got closer to the car, he began to skid a little. As I watched this happen, I got tenser every second. Then what I feared most happened. He collided into my car, stone-filled hand first, and scraped a little of the paint off my lovely, steel-blue import.

"Toby!" I yelled hysterically. "Look at my car. Oh,

my car! My car!" I was almost weeping with rage. "Get in the house!" I screamed. "Get in the house! Go on. *Now!*"

My son just stood there, frozen to the spot in fear. His knees trembled, and he sniffed. Tiny tears rolled down his cheeks.

"Did you hear me? Get in that house, now!" Sobbing now, his eyes and face red from the tears, that little three-year old whom I love so dearly ran down the walk and into our home.

I stood there for a second while the shock of what had happened waned slowly from my body. Gradually, I began to come back to my senses. How could I have screamed so much at my own sweet, little three-year old over an inanimate piece of metal, chrome, and rubber, I thought. But I did. In that moment I realized how much that car really meant to me. It meant more to me, obviously, than my own sweet son.

Now, if you had asked me before that incident about the worth of that car, I would have said, "The car means nothing to me. God can take it any time He wants to." But then God sent a little ambassador to me and said, "I want some of the paint from your car," and what happened? I exploded.

In order to help me become a stronger Christian, God used the heat of that circumstance to cause the sinful attitude inside me to rise to the surface so it could be dealt with and blown away.

In the same way, God will allow the circumstances in your life to purify you. He'll let them heat up to such an intense degree that the dross inside of you comes to the surface. Then, when it is exposed, He'll blow across it by His Spirit. In the end, you'll be stronger and purer, a clearer reflection of Christ to the world.

The Master's Threshing Floor

God also has another way of refining you and making you more like Jesus. It's called *winnowing*. In Matthew 3:12, John the Baptist says this of Christ:

> And His winnowing fork is in His hand,
> and He will thoroughly clean His threshing
> floor; and He will gather His wheat into the
> barn, but He will burn up the chaff with un-
> quenchable fire.

A winnowing fork is an instrument a farmer uses to process raw wheat into a substance that can finally be used to make bread.

The farmer takes wheat from the field and lays it down on what is called a threshing floor. Then he beats the wheat with sticks, stomps on it with his feet, and rolls over it with logs, shaking, stretching, and flattening it out. Next he takes his winnowing fork and throws the wheat into the air. As it's tossed, a wind blows through it, separating the precious wheat from the chaff.

Have you been feeling as though you're beaten down, rolled over with the logs of life, and stomped on? Have broken relationships and negative emotional experiences left you shaken, uprooted, and beaten down? Do you feel as though nothing is tied down in your life? If you're on shaky ground, it's an unsettling feeling. But I want you to know that if you respond rightly to these situations, you're going to grow in God and

44

become more conformed to the image of His Son.

God has allowed these situations to come upon your life so you may be purified and ultimately become bread to feed a hungry world. He's allowed you to experience the rigors of single living. He's allowed you to go through the pain of separation and rejection. He's allowed it so that you might be more closely conformed to the image of His Son.

But many singles don't understand the dealings that God brings into their life. "Why would God allow that divorce to go through, if He really loved me? Why would He let my husband die? Why would He let me experience that abusive relationship? Why would He allow me to be alone and lonely? Why would He allow my engagement to be broken?" they ask. Then, despondent, discouraged, and even *angry* at God, they run away from those situations rather than allow them to help them be conformed to the image of His Son, as He intended.

Following are five forms of testing the Lord uses to purify and strengthen you to make you more like Christ. I believe that by understanding them you will be better able to respond to them in a fruitful way and grow, as God intends you to, into a purer reflection of Christ.

The Wilderness Test

Have you ever been in a place with the Lord where you were stretched to your human limit? Your kids were having some mega-sized problem involving school friends. Your job was requiring more of you than you had to give. Yet, as you looked at your life, you knew

man does not live by bread alone, but man
lives by everything that proceeds out of the
mouth of the Lord.

Out in the wilderness, the Israelites could do nothing
humanly to survive. This forced them to call upon the
Lord. When they did, they saw miracles happen. Manna
fell from the sky to feed them, and water sprang
from a rock.

God was teaching them to lean upon Him for their
sustenance and to rely on Him for their nourishment
and strength. He was teaching them, quite literally, that
even when they could accomplish nothing in a situation,
God could come through for them. He was
teaching them that victory in their lives did not come
from them but from Him alone.

Why did God want them to know that? Because He
wanted them to be able to respond rightly when He
brought them into the Promised Land. He wanted them
to know it was He, and He alone, who provided; and
He knew that if they didn't learn this principle *before*
they received their blessings, their chances for
backsliding were great, if not guaranteed. That's why,
in that same chapter (verses 11-14) Moses warned,

Beware lest you forget the Lord your God
by not keeping His commandments and His
ordinances and His statutes which I am com-
manding you today; lest, when you have
eaten and are satisfied, and have built good
houses and lived in them, and when your
herds and your flocks multiply, and your
silver and gold multiply, and all that you

have multiplies, then your heart becomes proud, and you forget the Lord your God who brought you out of Egypt, out of the house of slavery.

God wanted Israel to depend on Him, not on themselves. He wanted them to know, beyond a shadow of a doubt, that it was not their strength or ability that won them the Promised Land but God and God alone.

As you follow the Lord, God will bring you into your own wilderness. You will be faced with a situation—perhaps in your home, with your family, on the job, or at church. God will speak a word to you, and you will step out in faith, only to find your human resources are not enough to help you survive. You won't have the talent, the ability, or the finances. You'll be up against the wall. If God doesn't bail you out, you will just wither away.

God will bring you to that place for a purpose. He wants to teach you to rely on Him. He wants to teach you to call upon Him. He wants you to realize that He is your provider.

Particularly as a single person, you have a unique opportunity to see the fruit of this kind of testing. As a single person, there's a lot of tendency to depend on yourself. Without a spouse, a lot of responsibility falls on your shoulders. You have to see that bills are paid. You have to see that the kids are clothed and given schooling and health care. You have to see that they're given spiritual teaching and guidance. Even without kids, the responsibilities are still shouldered by only one person—you. You have to make sure the car is registered, inspected, and repaired. No one will be there to remind you. You have to see to it that you're adequately nourished. You have to make sure the rent is paid. *All* of it is your responsibility.

Because of this, it's easy, without even meaning to, to depend on yourself without allowing God to move in your behalf and show He can be trusted to provide.

But, sooner or later, you will reach the end of your rope. Perhaps you're thinking to yourself, Mike, I've already reached that point. I'm there now. I might even be a little bit beyond it. I've gotten to the point where I'm just barely scraping by, day by day. It's agonizing.

I want you to know that God has brought you to this point for a purpose. He wants you to stop trusting in the arm of the flesh and begin trusting in Him. He wants you to recognize that your whole life—from your spiritual walk to the food on your table—depends upon Him.

God has brought you to this place of need so you may call upon Him and find Him faithful to provide. God has brought you to this place of loneliness so you may find comfort and wholeness in Him. God has brought you to this point of sexual weakness so you may find strength to overcome in Him. God has brought you to this point of frustration in dealing with your children so you may find words of counsel, compassion, forgiveness, and correction in Him. God has brought you to this point of discouragement and frustration in your job so you may find encouragement, wisdom, and strength to persevere in Him. God has allowed you to be single now so you may find your fulfillment, not in another human being but in Him, its only true source.

In the wilderness, you learn to depend on God—even in the most dire circumstances. In doing so, you find strength for your life and put yourself on solid ground with Him. Then, when the blessings come—and God promises they will—you will know it is from the Lord, not yourself.

The Test Of Total Commitment

Another type of testing God uses to purify us is the Test Of Total Commitment. In this test, God challenges us to lay down everything we have and follow Him.

Have you ever been in a situation where God asked you to give up something you loved very much? Did He ever put His finger down on one area of your life and say, "Surrender that thing to me?" If you've been a Christian for any period of time, I'm sure God has done that. You can't go very far in your Christian walk without experiencing this purifying process. Just giving your life to Christ involves this kind of test. You must choose between your sinful life and the Christian walk.

But, as we walk farther down the road with Christ, the refinement continues. God has a call upon our lives. He wants to hold first place in our hearts. So every time something exalts itself above Him—every time there's something inside us that rivals with God for our attention—He'll ask us to give that thing to Him.

With Abraham, it was his only son, Isaac. With the rich young ruler, it was his material possessions. With you, it may be different. Perhaps, for you, it's a relationship. That's a common—and major—one for singles. Perhaps it's your right to control your children's destiny. Perhaps it's your right to have a comfortable place to live. But whatever it is, it causes you to be double-minded in your pursuit of God. You want to follow God, yes. But there's something else you desire, as well—something you're not willing to relinquish.

The problem is that if you don't let go of it, it will keep you from being fulfilled as a child of God and from growing in Him. It will prevent you from being formed, any further, into the image of His Son. It may even cause you to backslide.

Once I knew a young woman whom God used powerfully—especially among single people. Head of a vibrant, successful singles ministry at her local church, she had spoken at several of our earlier retreats.

Not long ago, I called the lady's church to see if she would speak at another conference. The pastor got on the phone. "Mike, she's not coming to church here any more." I was stunned by the news. "Not going to church there? What do you mean? Six months ago. . . ."

"Well, not any more," he said and began to unravel a sad tale for me. "It began with a man she met at work. This man was not a Christian, but she began developing a relationship with him anyway.

"At first I said nothing. I knew she understood she should not be unequally yoked with an unbeliever and hoped the relationship would wind down without my input. Unfortunately, it didn't."

Weeks turned into months, and still no sign of a breakup was in sight. The pastor's concern grew. This woman was not only endangering herself but giving a wrong kind of witness to the singles she led. He knew he had to confront her.

A few days later, they met in his office. "I've noticed

you're seeing this man," he began as delicately as he could. "And I know he's not a Christian. As for you, you're a singles leader. You know you shouldn't be seeing this person. In fact, I was hoping you'd stop seeing him on your own. But you haven't. Now I feel I have to ask you—and this is very hard for me to do—to break off your relationship with him or step down...."

One mention of discontinuing the relationship was enough to set her off. "This man is better than any Christian man I have ever met," she said, becoming almost livid. "So, if you're saying I can't lead the singles ministry anymore if I continue to see him, then I guess I won't be involved in the ministry anymore." And from that day on, she wasn't.

For awhile she kept coming to services on Sundays; but, gradually, that stopped, too. "For all I know," the pastor said with a sigh, "she's fallen away from Christ by now and has backslidden."

"What happened to her?" I wondered aloud. "How could someone so on fire for God fall away so quickly and so finally?"

"I guess," the pastor said, "she never really yielded her right to marriage to the Lord."

In this woman's life was a desire for marriage that countered her desire for God. It was a strong desire, but one she kept buried, for the most part, in the deepest recesses of her heart. There, deep within her, that desire took root and grew, until one day it was too big to keep buried. It surged to the surface and took control, claiming first place in her heart.

Then, when she was confronted with a decision, she chose her relationship with that man over her relationship with Jesus Christ.

That's the chance you take when you continue to covet something strongly and are not willing to relinquish it to God. Just the fact that you have trouble releasing it to Him shows you the power it exudes in your life and the place it has in your heart. *It's more important to you than God Himself.*

God knows the danger of having a desire like that in your heart. He knows that, when the pressure is on, that desire inside you could cause you to fall away from Him. So God calls upon you—gently but persistently— to yield that thing to Him. Oh, you can put it off, but every time you try to go forward in God, that same issue will come to the surface—maybe not at first, but eventually. God will point to it patiently and say, as He did to Abraham, "Take your one, your only, and offer it to Me." It's the Test Of Total Commitment, which, when submitted to, will open the door to massive growth in your Christian life.

The Old Enemy Test

Have you ever seen the transforming power of God operate in the life of an unbeliever with, by human standards, really horrible problems and sin—a drug addict, a prostitute, or perhaps a drunk? One minute, they're the vilest person you've ever met; and the next, having accepted Jesus as their Lord and Savior, they're made completely pure—not even a foul word coming out of their mouth. Their lives have been radically changed. In an instant, they're made holy.

That's an amazing and exciting thing to witness. But have you ever wondered why the power of God is able to do that for them, yet you're left struggling with sins that beat you down day after day after day? He's given you that same power. Why do they experience such immediate victory while you are left doing battle with some sins for years and years?

I know I wondered about that. I'd look at my life and see certain besetting sins that, try as hard as I might, just refused to die in my life. I'd look at them, then at what God had done for others, and say, "Lord, if you can clean up people like that in an instant, why are these things still in my life? Why don't you just take care of them? Why don't you just take them away?"

Then, one day, I was reading the book of Judges, and I came across this passage in Chapter 3:1-2:

> Now these are the nations which the Lord left, to test Israel by them (that is, all who had not experienced any of the wars of Canaan; only in order that the generations of the sons of Israel might be taught war, those who had not experienced it formerly).

The passage nearly jumped off the page at me. Immediately, I began to see God's purpose in allowing me to struggle with those besetting sins. He wanted me to learn to do battle with them so I could become strong and victorious in Him. He wanted me to "be taught war. . .who had not experienced it formerly."

You are probably struggling with certain things in your life. Perhaps it's sexual desires; perhaps a fear of relationships; perhaps a habit of smoking; or eating too much; or thinking negatively all the time. You've fought with that thing so many times that you're almost ready to quit. In fact, there have been times when you've given in. "That's it. I quit. You win. Walk over me." You've gotten up and been beaten down by that thing so many times that you just can't live with the battle any more.

You've prayed many times that it would go away. "If I could just get rid of this thing," you've thought, "I could really do something for God." But the truth is that God left that thing in your life so you *could* do something for God. You see, it's in doing battle, learning to war with the old enemies in your life, and—in God—finding victory over them that you'll become strong and do exploits for God. It's in learning how to conquer a debilitating fear, a strong sexual urge, or a tendency to fly off in anger that you'll be purified and strengthened in God. You'll learn how to fight. You'll learn how to conquer.

God has places for you to conquer. Did you know that? He has places for you to rule and reign over beyond your imagination. God has said we will sit with Him in heavenly places and claim the whole of creation for Him.

I believe that is what heaven is all about. I believe that eternity is not going to be spent sitting around strumming harps. I believe we're going to rule entire planets, solar systems, and galaxies beyond our imaginations in Jesus' name. We're going to go forth to do battle for our Lord and bring everything under His dominion.

But He can't do it with a lot of wimps. He needs people who have learned war. He needs people trained for battle, willing to persevere even against the toughest foes. That's why He's allowing you to go through the old enemy test right now. That's why He's allowing the struggles of your singleness to remain—so you can learn to wrestle, fight, do battle, and conquer in the power of your Lord, Jesus Christ.

Are you struggling today with some besetting sin or weakness? Don't be ashamed. That battleground is your place of training. You're being trained to fight the good fight so you can reign with Him in heavenly places.

Test Of The Unfulfilled Word Of The Lord

Has God ever spoken a word into your life, but you've never seen its fulfillment? Perhaps you felt the call to be a leader in your local church. Perhaps God was speaking to you about becoming a pastor, an evangelist, a prophet, or a teacher. Perhaps He was giving you visions of leadership in the business community, in social services, or in a creative field. As God unfolded His plan before you, you became excited.

But now, the months and the years have gone by, and nothing seems to have happened. You're *sure* the Lord spoke to you, for undeniable recognition resounded in your heart. Yet, everything in your life seems to indicate that vision will never come to pass. You're still sitting in the pew of that big congregation and setting up chairs on Sunday. You're still just another cog in the wheel at your firm. You're still typing letters rather than being at the helm of that publication God has laid on your heart. You're still serving coffee in the church basement rather than speaking the Word in front of the congregation as God said you would. Perhaps you've begun the journey, only to experience a series of frustrations and failures. Maybe the doors have been slammed in your face over and over again. You see no indication that God's vision is going to come to pass.

Joseph would understand what you are going through. God gave Him a big vision, too. He said his own brothers would come and bow down before him. The Lord told Joseph he would be a leader of his people. Yet here he was, a little shepherd boy thrown into a well by his brothers—then sold into slavery, and finally thrown into jail. He suffered one discouragement after another. Why? What was happening? Psalm 105:16-19 takes a look at the situation:

> And He called for a famine upon the land; He broke the whole staff of bread. He sent a man before them, Joseph, who was sold as a slave. They afflicted his feet with fetters, He himself was laid in irons; Until the time that his word came to pass, the word of the Lord tested him.

God spoke a word into Joseph's heart. Joseph knew that word was true. Even when his brothers grew angry, threw him in a hole, and sold him into slavery, he knew. Even when he was falsely accused of attempted rape by Potiphar's wife and thrown in jail, he knew. Even when the prisoners he helped didn't remember to intercede for his freedom, he knew. Despite all the circumstances that spoke messages to the contrary, Joseph believed God, and it acted as a refiner in his life, purifying and strengthening him in his walk with God.

Imagine yourself in Joseph's place. God has given you a vision: Your brothers are going to bow down to you. Then, what happens? Your brothers throw you in a hole and stand over it, looking in at you. You have two choices at this point. You can get discouraged and allow doubt and unbelief to creep in. "This isn't the way God said it would be. Maybe I heard Him wrong. Maybe He didn't give me that vision, after all." Or you can proceed in faith, standing on the word. "God said it. I believe it. That settles it."

What happens when you choose to walk in faith? All the thoughts, feelings, and attitudes that try to come against that stance are forced to fall away. You become purified and strengthened in your faith, and your eyes are more firmly focused on the Lord and what He wants to accomplish in you.

Then imagine yourself as Potiphar's right-hand man. Everything's going well. You're the boss' favorite. He can count on you. You've earned his trust by serving him with excellence, doing every task, however large or small, to the best of your ability. Then one day his wife begins to pursue you in an unwholesome way. You don't want to transgress the trust placed in you by your boss; and, being a Christian, you certainly don't want to offend God. So you avoid her. But she keeps it up, pursuing you whenever she gets the chance. Finally, when she sees you're not going to give in, she gets mad and decides to get revenge. She tells Potiphar you tried to rape her, and he throws you in jail. Not only are you a slave, but you're an imprisoned one.

Again, you've got two choices. You can become embittered: "How could she lie about me? How could Potiphar believe her? It isn't fair. It isn't right." Or you can do what Joseph did: Submit to the situation, continue to believe God, and become the best prisoner you can be, so God will be glorified.

Since Joseph chose to submit, the circumstances he faced were able to purify him. He was able to learn humility and servanthood and to be available to help others, even in the most dire circumstances. His eyes were focused all the more on the Lord, and he was trained in faith amid all circumstances. Even in what could have been the deepest, darkest, most discouraging moments of his life, Joseph grew in God and bore fruit.

In the same way, God will allow you to be tested as you wait for the fulfillment of His Word to you. Yes, at times you will look around and the vision will seem anything but near. But if you will submit to each situation you find yourself in—if you will yield those circumstances that could be frustrating, depressing, discouraging, even defeating to Him and believe His Word to you in the midst of them—God will use them to purify and strengthen you, making you more like His Son day by day.

The Test Of No Sense Of The Presence Of God

Do you know what it is to be left alone by God? Do you know what it feels like to come into a service where the power of God is moving and feel absolutely nothing at all? All around you people are getting stirred by the pastor's message. You can see it in their eyes. Afterward, many are talking about the sermon. But there is no response inside of you. You feel nothing, even though you know you should. The message has left you dead.

This happened to me when I was in Bible school. I lost the conscious sense of the presence of God. I went to chapel services every day, sang hymns, and listened to sermons. Afterward, the whole student body would be buzzing about what they had gotten out of the service. But not me. I would go in, sing, and listen. But I received nothing. The hymns didn't stir me, and the words of the sermon didn't speak to my heart. I felt nothing at all. I was dry. This really bothered me. God had given me a call to preach, and here I was, not even stirred by the Word. I hoped it would change and that the fire would return. But it didn't. The weeks rolled by, and I remained unmoved.

Finally, Christmas break came. I felt I had to make a decision. God surely doesn't want preachers like me, I thought. Not people this deadened, dried out, and unresponsive to His Word. So I decided to go home for the holidays and never come back.

Well, I went home and went to church—not because I wanted to but because I felt it was my duty and obligation to do so. I remember how everyone ran up to greet me. "How is Bible school?" they asked enthusiastically. (Everyone thinks Bible school is heaven on earth.) I didn't know what to say. How could I tell them what I was feeling? How could I say I felt nothing at all? How could I tell them I was thinking of quitting school altogether? I didn't want to be sour, so I just made some noncommittal statement, like, "Oh, yeah, well, really, it's never been like this before," and basically kept my mouth shut.

During the holidays, the church had a special speaker come to minister. She was an extremely gifted woman, sensitive to the movement of the Spirit. Everyone got excited and planned to attend. But within me there was only hesitancy. I had heard much about this woman's ministry and how she spoke to the innermost needs in people, but I feared that even this would leave me dry. What if I go and still don't sense the presence of God? I thought.

Yet, despite my feelings and fears, I decided to go. I listened as she spoke to the congregation. The words were right in accordance with Scripture. People around me were stirred by the message, but nothing happened to me. God, as far as I could tell, was nowhere to be found.

After her message, some people went forward for prayer. I watched as she prayed with them. Some even had tears in their eyes as she prayed. How I longed for God to touch me like that. It had happened to me before, but it seemed like such a long time ago. I stood to leave, and as I did, the visiting minister caught my eye and waved me forward with her hand.

"Oh, no. She wants to pray with me. Oh, no. I'm going to be exposed. Now she'll know how dead I am. It'll be so noticeable." Reluctantly, I moved toward her. Then she began to pray: "You have prayed, and it has seemed to you as though the heavens were brass. You have cried out to God, and you have said, 'Come to me. Help me. Come to me where I am.' But God cannot come to you where you are. *You* have to come to Him. If He met you where you were, you would stay there; you wouldn't move on. So He, as your loving Father, has held Himself back from you. He has shut His ears to your cries that you might long for Him and go forward in Him. And now He calls you to come to Him."

Tears rolled down my cheeks as she spoke. For the first time in months I could feel His presence, and I knew the words she spoke were important ones for me. Even as I had heard them, I realized what had gone wrong in my relationship with God. I had created a place of comfort for myself. Reaching a certain plateau of spiritual experience, I had settled down. I felt so good there, so at ease. Everything was so right. But while I sat in that place of comfort, God left. He moved on.

Let me tell you, nobody plans on losing God. I sure didn't. Neither did Mary and Joseph. When they left the feast at Jerusalem, they didn't look around for Jesus. They just assumed He was with their group somewhere.

That's the way we are sometimes, too. We set up a little place of security, start doing something in our church, get involved in our own little projects, and *assume* He's there with us all along. But He's not. He's gone. He leaves.

A few years ago, an uncomfortable incident happened to me while I was clothes shopping with my son, Toby, who was then three years old. Like all little kids, Toby liked to play in the clothes racks whenever we went shopping. He'd hide himself in those racks and walk around getting his head inside all the clothes.

One day we were out together, and I was looking for some pants. As usual, Toby was getting into the racks. From time to time, I would look down, find him, and tell him to get out. Well, as often happens when you're absorbed in clothes shopping, I got caught up examining some pairs of pants to see how well they were made, whether I thought the color was something I liked, what they cost, and so on. After looking at a few pairs but finding nothing I wanted, I decided to leave the store. I called to my son. "Ok, Toby. We're ready to go. Come on." No answer. "Toby, come on. We're going now." Still no reply. I listened for a rustle of clothes in one of the nearby racks. Nothing. Slowly, I began walking up and down the aisles, lifting up clothes, parting hangers, and discreetly calling his name. There was no sign of him anywhere.

"Toby," I said, a little louder. "Toby." I was getting tense now but still trying to cover it. "Excuse me," I said, tapping a mild-looking, middle-aged lady on the shoulder. "Uh, have you seen a . . . little boy. He'a about so high. Blond hair. Little red shirt, blue pants? Toby! Toby!" My pitch was getting higher now. By this time, I had searched the whole department. He was nowhere to be found. "God, where is he?"

I picked up my pace and began jogging around the store, screaming his name. I didn't care what I looked like now. All I wanted to do was find my little boy. "Toby! *Toby!*"

I ran up to a customer service desk, my eyes bulging with anxiety. "Have you seen a little boy?"

"You'll find him. You'll find him . . ." the lady behind the desk said quietly, trying to reassure me. By this time people were running all over the store.

Suddenly, out of the mall entrance came a woman. She had my son by the hand, and she was looking at me as if to say, "You call yourself a parent?" I felt bad, but I was so glad to see my son, I almost didn't care. "Oh, my son, my son. You found him. Oh, thank you, thank you, thank you. Toby, my son, my son. I'm so glad to see you." Then, a little sternly, "Don't *ever* do that again. Stay near your father."

Now, I never went into that store intending to lose my son, but I did. Similarly, nobody intends to lose

63

God. But they do. They get involved in something and get ready to go, when, all of a sudden, they realize He's not there.

At first they try to remain calm. "God . . . hello, God. I know you're there. God?" But there's no answer. We try again. "God, I'm calling to you. Come here, God. Come here." Still no reply. Then we panic. "Jesus . . . why isn't it like it used to be? Where *are* you? Why aren't you here? Please, come back. Please come here."

But He can't come to you. Like a loving father, He's holding Himself back so He can call you to Himself.

Today, if you're in a place where you can't sense God as you used to, He is calling you to come to Him. Don't stay where you are. Don't say it has to be your way. Don't ask Him to meet you where you are. Go to Him. Follow Him, and keep your eye on Him. That's what He's trying to teach you. He's trying to show you the importance of following Him, as Christ did, and of hearing and responding to His call.

Perhaps you've been looking at the testings of God in your own life as you've been reading this. Maybe you haven't been feeling His presence. Maybe you've been feeling tossed in the air, without roots. Perhaps you've been struggling with the same old problems that have plagued you for years. You may have been asked to surrender something and follow Him. Or perhaps you're struggling with an unfulfilled word.

But I want you to know something. These testings have come for a purpose—not to cause you to faint or give up but to form you into the image of Jesus Christ, the Son of God.

If you will allow them, these testings can be more

than trials endured. They can be stepping stones of Christian growth, paving the way to make you more productive for Christ.

Chapter Three

SINGLENESS DOESN'T MEAN REJECTION

Singleness doesn't mean rejection.

Many single people labor under the false concept that their status in life is a sign of rejection. They look at their singleness—whether caused by divorce, a broken engagement, or never having been in a relationship that led to marriage—and see it as a stigma on their life, almost akin to a highly contagious, socially unacceptable disease. "I'm a reject. I'm no good. I'm a nobody. If I were somebody—if there were *anything* attractive in me—then I'd be married."

To be honest, many of them, especially the divorced and the never-married, can look into their past and point to incidents of deep rejection—people treated them as worthless or never even gave them a chance.

But just being rejected does not make a person "a reject," worthless, or some kind of leftover in life.

Singleness is neither a stigma nor a social disease. It's a matter of *choice*. "What! Mike, how can you say that? I'm divorced. I'm widowed. My fiancee broke off our engagement. I never wanted this lonely life. Not ever. How can you tell me I'm single because I've chosen to be?"

Because it's true. Oh, you may not have become single in the first place because you chose to be. Someone else may have gotten the divorce. Someone else may have broken the engagement. Someone else may have died. But, right now, as you are reading this book, you *are* single by choice. Let me explain to you what I mean.

If you wanted to be married today, you could be. I guarantee you, I could find somebody for you. If you had no criteria, no real guidelines, or no moral standards to speak of, I could find someone who'd be willing to marry you. Anybody who doesn't have any standards can get married.

But you *do* have standards; and, whether or not the idea is comfortable for you, you're single because of those standards. You've made certain choices in your life. Some of them may have been good, and others may have been bad. That matters little. The fact is you chose them. You're single by choice.

Even your choice to be a Christian has narrowed the field. As a Christian, you've made a lot of choices that non-Christian singles haven't. You're not of this world, and you don't follow their standards. You've chosen to follow Christ, and it has set you apart. It has limited your choices.

Let me give you a few examples. You don't go to some of the places that non-Christian singles go. You don't think along the same lines as non-Christian singles do. You don't even approach your work and your relationships with others the way they do. And that's because of a choice you've made. A choice for life—a choice for Jesus Christ.

That's why a lot of you are single today. You're single

because of Christ. You're single because you haven't been willing to compromise the Truth you stand for. You're single for God. And on the day you stand before Him, He's not going to look at you and rate you on your marital status. He's not going to say, "Oh, poor Janie. Somehow she just never made it to the altar. She just didn't make it." He's going to look into your heart and see the uncompromising stand you took, with the desire of being wholly pleasing to Him. He's going to see your singleness not as a failure but as the price you were willing to pay to follow Him.

You've chosen to be single. It's not some evil curse, and it's not a sign you've failed. If anything, it's a sign you've chosen Jesus as your Lord and Savior, and you stand for righteousness. That's a fantastic choice, indeed, and a great reason for being single. *You're single for Him!*

But that doesn't mean, instantly, you're going to be a whole person, completely repaired—and freed—from the pain of past rejections and hurts. In fact, the rejections you've suffered can actually keep you from experiencing the full life you can have as a Christian single, redeemed by God.

However, there is a biblical program I'd like to share with you for overcoming the rejections you've suffered and the hurts that keep you from experiencing that full life in Christ.

To uncover it, we need to go to the heart of the Gospel:

> Who has believed our message? And to whom has the arm of the Lord been revealed? For He grew up before Him like a

tender shoot, and like a root out of parchedground; He has no stately form or majesty that we should look upon Him, nor appearance that we should be attracted to Him. He was despised and forsaken of men, a man of sorrows, and acquainted with grief; and like one from whom men hide their face, He was despised, and we did not esteem Him. Surely our griefs He Himself bore, and our sorrows He carried; yet we ourselves esteemed Him stricken, smitten of God, and afflicted. But He was pierced through for our transgressions, He was crushed for our iniquities; the chastening for our well-being fell upon Him, and by His scourging we are healed. All of us like sheep have gone astray, each of us has turned to his own way; but the Lord has caused the iniquity of us all to fall on Him . . . .But the Lord was pleased to crush Him, putting Him to grief (Isaiah 53:1-6,10).

How well we know these verses. They testify of the salvation work of Jesus, who died once to free us from sin and restore us to fellowship with the Father. ''He made Him who knew no sin to be sin on our behalf,that we might become the righteousness of God in Him'' (2 Corinthians 5:21). Yes, we understand it well enough; but how often we live as though it had never happened.

How often have you said to yourself, after having done something wrong, ''Oh, no. Look what I did. It'll be *days* before I can come into God's presence again,'' then sentenced yourself to a self-imposed exile from the presence of God? If you're like others, you've done this probably more times than you care to remember. Do you know how that breaks His heart? I do.

Once when I was associate pastor of a local church, I got an intense desire to experience God face to face. I had read in the Old Testament that Moses had such an experience, so I thought, How much more should I be able to experience something like that as a New Testament believer. So, one day, I began praying to God for such an experience. "Oh God," I prayed, "I want to know you as Moses did. I want to know you face to face. Reveal yourself to me."

As I prayed, the presence of God began to fill the room. It flowed into every corner and built in intensity. A warm, liquid presence of Him rested everywhere. It was incredible.

Then, in a flash, I realized what had begun to happen. I knew God was about to manifest Himself to me in all His glory, and suddenly I grew afraid. I blurted out, "No! Don't do it!" In a second the presence was gone, quickly and suddenly.

I sat in my room and wept, conscious of having shut God out. Then He spoke to me: "Mike, why are you afraid of Me?"

I said, "God, there are some awfully wrong things in my life. It's one thing to talk about seeing You and knowing You in a face-to-face way. But I'm no Moses. I've got some things in my life I'd be ashamed to show You. I'd be ashamed to look into Your face."

Then God spoke a word to my heart that has affected me ever since. He said, "Michael, your sin already separated me from Somebody I loved very much. When you turned away, it separated Me twice.''

When God allowed His Son to die on the cross for our sins, the act was permanent. From now on we who are saved never have to be separated from God again. It's why He paid the price. Yet, continually, we live as though that provision were not made. We act as though we must still pay the price. That's very sad because it's already paid in full.

But Jesus bore more than our sins on that day. Isaiah 53 says He bore our hurts and rejections as well. He took them all on Himself so we could be free.

The Cross Is An Exchange

Because of Jesus, we can exchange our rejections for His acceptance. We can exchange our hurts for His healing, His peace, and His joy. I want to show you how.

The first thing I want to deal with is *rejection*. I think I'm well acquainted with rejection. Since I grew up in a home without a father, I had to do many things myself that other boys got to do with their dads. If I wanted to take up a sport, for instance, I had to make all my own arrangements. I had no father to sign me up or talk to the appropriate people for me.

One thing I wanted to do badly when I was small was play Little League baseball. I knew tryouts in my home town were coming up, so I managed to get myself a glove and find some neighborhood kids to practice with.

I practiced every chance I got. Wherever kids were playing baseball, you would find me. I was out there with them.

Finally, the day of tryouts came; and, because we

72

didn't own a car, I had to find another way to get there. So I walked. It was a long walk—more than two miles. But I wanted to be in Little League more than anything else.

When I arrived at the field, I saw fathers and sons practicing and waiting their turn to try out. All over the diamond, boys were running, catching, and pitching. Being just a boy, I wasn't sure of the procedures, so I got out on the diamond and joined in.

You never saw anyone who put more heart into their tryout than I did. I pitched with all the strength in my little arm. I caught high pops. I fielded. I ran as fast as I could. And all the while I hoped one of the coaches would notice me. I didn't have a father to point me out: "Hey, did you see that kid catch that high fly ball to center? That's my boy, Mike." I just had to hope my performance would speak for me.

As dusk settled on the ballpark, the coaches took their pads in hand and began reading out the names of those who'd made the league. Team after team was called, name after name. I strained to hear my own. I never did.

Perhaps there was some form to sign I didn't know about. Perhaps I had to introduce myself to someone. I don't know. All I do know is that I felt rejected, and the little boy heart inside me was shattered. But being such a small child, I didn't know how to handle that hurt. So I just shoved it deep down within my being and went on. But unconsciously, I made a decision: I would never go near sports again.

Years later, when I was in high school, that unconscious vow I'd made still remained in effect. I loathed anything to do with sports, but I didn't know why. I'd skip gym class, and I didn't care. Even if they threatened to take me out of school, I still wouldn't go. I just hated anything to do with sports, all because of a wall I had unconsciously built during my childhood.

Although I became a Christian in my senior year of high school, my strong dislike for sports remained. I wouldn't even watch them on television. It was that bad.

Then one day, over five years later, circumstances forced me to confront the feelings deep inside. I was associate pastor of a local church at the time.

Some of the men from the church decided to start a softball team, and they asked me to join. "Come on, Mike. You've *got* to be a part of it. It's going to be great."

Suddenly, inside of me, a great surge of resistance arose. "No, I don't want to. I just don't like sports. Really." But they insisted, so I gave in. After all, I *was* associate pastor of the church. I *should* get involved, even if it *wasn't* my thing. Reluctantly, I went out, got a mitt, and began practicing my skills again.

Then the day of the first game came. I felt a little nauseated and nervous inside. It was a weird reaction, and I didn't understand why I felt so strange. I didn't know the wall I had unconsciously built as a child still stood inside me.

Sensing my reluctance and tension, the men put me out in right field. If you know anything about right field, you know it's the place the baseball almost never goes. It's where you put the low man on the team.

So there I was in right field, the tension and anxiety

mounting. Then the game began. Occasionally, a ball would come in my direction and—to my shock and delight—I'd catch it. This happened a few times, until, eventually, I began to get excited. Not just a little thrilled, mind you, but way-out excited, beyond comprehension. I didn't understand it. I wasn't doing too much—just catching the ball now and then. But every time I did so, I experienced a surge of emotion. I imagined myself catching a high fly ball. I heard the crowds—all three bleachers of kids and wives— shouting and screaming. It was an inordinate reaction, and I didn't understand it at all. But I knew one thing for sure: I was really *enjoying* myself.

That night, I got home and began to pray. "God, what was that all about? Why did I get so thrilled about such an ordinary thing?" That's when He reminded me about the rejection from Little League many years before. "Mike," God said, "for years you've carried the rejection you suffered as a child in your heart. It's kept you out of every kind of sport and even caused you to keep from watching it or reading about it. But today on that field, for the first time in your life, you were laying the rejection of the past on Me, and you were free."

That was a thrilling moment for me. I realized for the first time what God had done for me through His Son Jesus Christ. He had shouldered the rejection of my childhood upon Himself so I could find freedom from pain and fullness of joy in my life with Him, right down to an activity like baseball.

Perhaps you've had some deep rejections in your life and, like me, you've built walls to protect yourself from ever experiencing them again. Some you consciously remember building—others you don't remember. But that matters little. What I want you to know is this— you can be free from that wall today. Right now, you can come out from behind that wall, take the fear of rejection—whether a result of that painful divorce, that broken engagement, or those unfulfilled relationships—and lay it upon Jesus Christ. You can take the rejections of childhood that have caused you to build walls between yourself and others and lay them upon Him now. You can lay everything that has ever held you back or made you feel unlovely upon Him and find healing, freedom, and joy.

Won't you do that *right now?* Take that rejection of your spouse to Jesus. Take that break-up with your fiancee to Jesus. Take the wounds of your childhood to Christ, and lay them upon Him—He will set you free.

Supernatural Release

Another thing Christ bore on the cross for you is *grief or sorrow.*

I used to have a habit of laughing at tragic things. For example, if someone told me about a fifteen-car pile-up on Route 69, I would picture all these people hanging out their windows ogling the scene, while a bunch of others ran around, comically hysterical, like characters out of a Three Stooges film. And I would laugh. It was really strange.

Once, while I was in Bible school, I began telling a rather sad story to a girlfriend of mine. It involved a chick-hatching project I had done in grammar school.

The project required me to keep a close watch over some eggs and make sure they hatched without problem. I took my responsibilities seriously. I watched those eggs vigilantly. When I couldn't be home, I made sure my mother watched them for me. They had to be turned at exact intervals, and I made sure they were— whether I did it or somebody else did it for me.

After a few weeks, the hatching process was almost over. Late one night, after most of the chicks had come out of their shells, I was carefully watching the last unhatched egg. I didn't want the chick to hatch when I wasn't looking because I feared it might burn itself on the heater that kept the incubator warm.

Unfortunately, I grew very tired. Try as hard as I might, I could not keep my eyes open. Eventually I dozed off, only to be awakened minutes later by a high peeping sound. It was the last chick. He had hatched and, as I feared, burnt himself on the heater.

As I told the girl the story, I began to recall how the little chick had to struggle to stand up straight because of his wound. Then, as soon as he was standing, one of the other chicks would run over and bump him until he fell down. Now, that's very sad, but I didn't cry. Instead, I laughed until my sides ached.

My girlfriend stared at me. "Mike, you're not really *laughing* about this, are you?" she asked. I got defensive. Something inside me knew she was hitting close to home. "What do you mean, I'm not really laughing? What are you, some kind of psychiatrist or something?" I couldn't let her know she had touched on a sensitive subject, yet her message had gone straight to my heart. I knew God was trying to point something out to me.

Later on, in my room, I knelt and prayed. "God, what did she mean, 'You're not really laughing?' What was she getting at?'' Then the Lord reminded me of an incident that happened to me in grammar school.

I was a super-sensitive kid in grammar school. Maybe it had something to do with my broken home life. I don't know. But I would cry at the drop of a hat. If something hurtful happened around me, I would weep. It didn't even have to involve me in any way.

One day in school the class bully began picking on the class scapegoat right in front of me. As I watched the poor guy take a verbal beating, I could feel the tears forming in my eyes. I knew I was going to cry, but I didn't want to do it in front of my classmates. So, even though I didn't really feel that way, I began to laugh, loud and hard, at that poor, defenseless kid.

I thought about the moment, running the scene over and over again through my mind. Then God began to speak: ''Mike, in that moment, you became your own defense. You became your own emotional shield, and you've never let it down. You've never let Me be your shield. You've never let Me be your protection. You've never let Me be your strong tower of defense.''

The next day I began to tell the same girl another sad story. As had happened the day before, I got to the tragic part and began to laugh. Again she stared at me and said, ''Mike, you're not *really laughing* about that, are you?''

''Wait a minute. Just wait a minute,'' I said. Then I covered my face and became quiet. I wanted to allow my true feelings to surface. Soon I was weeping. In that moment I knew, for the first time, that God had become my emotional shield, my protector, and my strong tower of defense, and I was free to express my true self.

Perhaps in your own life certain wounds have

caused you to build walls and put up smoke screens. Perhaps the pain of separation or divorce has caused you to stop being genuine with others. Every time you're around someone, particularly of the opposite sex, you put on a mask. It's *not* the real you. It's a protective shield to keep you from ever being hurt again.

God is saying to you today that you don't need those defenses any more. You don't need those masks. You've got a better one—the Lord Himself.

God desires for you to lay those defenses aside and trust completely in Him. He is calling you to take those hurts and release them to Him. God wants you to lay the wounds of that divorce, the anger of loss in widowhood, or the frustration and pain of multiple rejections that you may have experienced in the single life upon Him.

He has *borne* them for you so you may know healing, wholeness, release, and freedom to love again in Him.

Chapter Four

A GIFT FOR SERVICE

Your singleness is a gift from God for service.

As in no other time in your life, your season as a single person sets you free to serve God in a wholehearted and undistracted way. Unencumbered by many of the duties and responsibilities that go along with the married life, you are able to say "yes" to God in a dynamic way. You are free to throw yourself with abandon into the things of God—to know Him as you have never known Him before, to love Him in an intimate way, and to serve Him with all your heart, soul, mind, and strength—one hundred percent.

The apostle Paul, a single Christian, knew and appreciated this. He said in 1 Corinthians 7:32-35,

> But I want you to be free from concern. One who is unmarried is concerned about the things of the Lord, how he may please the Lord; but one who is married is concerned about the things of the world, how he may please his wife, and his interests are divided. And the woman who is unmarried, and the virgin, is concerned about the

things of the Lord, that she may be holy both in body and spirit; but one who is married is concerned about the things of the world, how she may please her husband. *And this I say for your own benefit; not to put a restraint upon you, but to promote what is seemly, and to secure undistracted devotion to the Lord* (italics added).

Let's look at that last verse because Paul shares with us the complete goal of his counsel to singles.

What is that goal? "To promote what is seemly (right, decent, expedient) and to secure undistracted devotion to the Lord." Paul is in no way saying that marriage is wrong. He is encouraging Christians to see the benefits of the single life and to spend it in total consecration and commitment to the Lord and His purposes. He urges singles to be devoted to the Lord and to give Him all of their attention, time, and talents.

As a single person, you have been given a unique opportunity to know God in the same special way Paul knew Him. He has given you a season in which you may know Him deeply, undistracted by any other concerns.

Just what does Paul mean by "undistracted devotion"? The Greek word for "undistracted" in this portion of text means "to be constantly attendant upon" or "to be sitting near." It's a servant's term, and it describes the kind of servant who is so focused on his master that just the slightest eye movement or gesture of need will send that servant into action. Let me show you what I mean.

A little while ago, I went to Dallas, Texas, to speak at a local church. As often happens, the pastor took me out to lunch after the service. We went to a Chinese restaurant.

Now this restaurant was *really* Chinese. It had red chairs, red walls, and red tablecloths. A hand-painted Chinese calendar hung on the wall behind the cash register and Chinese lanterns dangled from the ceiling. It was even staffed with Chinese hostesses, waitresses, and busboys.

Our waitress was an efficient woman, well versed in the English language. But our table attendant (the person who actually did all the serving) was a new immigrant and very Oriental in all of her ways. Still learning English, she was in that uncomfortable place of understanding a lot of what she heard but not wanting to respond. (She didn't want to make an awful mistake and be embarrassed by her own cumbersome handle on the new language.) So she just kept quiet and went about her business.

We ordered, and our attendant came around and filled our glasses with water. While we waited for our meal, the pastor and I passed the time chatting. My throat got a little dry, and I reached for my glass of water and took a sip.

Immediately, out of the corner of the room, our attendant shuffled over and refilled my glass. I thought, Well that's nice. . . . So I nodded at her, and she nodded at me. Then she toddled away.

I was impressed. Well, isn't that something, I

you had been obedient to God, insofar as you knew His will for you. So why the struggle? Why did He let it go so far? Why did He allow you to get to the end of your proverbial rope?

The answer, I believe, can be found in God's dealings with the children of Israel in the wilderness. Soon after they were freed by Pharaoh, the Israelites were led through the Red Sea. They watched as God provided a way of escape for them and destroyed their enemies in the process. So far so good. But what was on the other end of that sea waiting for them? The wilderness—a vast expanse of dry, arid land where water and food were difficult, if not downright impossible, to find.

It didn't take long for the Israelites to begin reminiscing about ''the good old days'' back in captivity when they always had enough to eat and drink. ''We had it good back there,'' they began to grumble. ''Now, since we've obeyed God, look at the problem we're in. We followed Him. We did what He told us to do. And now we're hungry and thirsty.''

Why would God do a thing like that to the Israelites? It doesn't seem to make a whole lot of sense. Why drag thousands of people out of a land where they were oppressed but fed, only to bring them to a place of drought and starvation? *To teach them dependence on Him.* In Deuteronomy 8:3, God's servant Moses explains:

> And He humbled you and let you be hungry, and fed you with manna which you did not know, nor did your fathers know, that He might make you understand that

thought. I didn't even have to say, "More water." I just drank a little bit, and she appeared immediately. What service!

The pastor and I talked a while longer, and the meal still hadn't arrived. I got thirsty again, so I reached over, grabbed my glass, and took another sip of water.

Immediately, the attendant ran over and filled my glass. I nodded to her once more. She nodded at me. I nodded again. She did the same. (This was getting ridiculous.) Finally, she walked away.

I shook my head in disbelief. In most restaurants, I practically had to start a fire in the ashtray to get anyone to come to my table. But here she was, running up to serve me at my slightest indication of need. I have to admit that I felt a little intimidated and found myself hesitating to take another drink for fear that she would feel obligated to come over again.

Finally the meal came, and I looked around the table for some salt. Well, this incredibly attentive woman noticed the slight movement of my head and came running over to see what I needed.

I can still remember her staring into my face with this look that said, "What do you want?" I said, "Salt," and she ran off and got me some. Isn't that incredible?

What I want you to see is this: that woman was *constantly* attendant upon me. I didn't need to speak. I didn't even need to signal. Just a slight movement of my head was enough to tell her I needed something.

That's exactly the way God wants you to respond to Him, too. He doesn't want to have to yell to you across the room: "Hey you! I need something." He wants you to be so attentive to Him that just the slightest movement of His eye will be able to prompt you to action.

84

Psalm 32:8-9 (KJV) says,

> I will instruct thee and teach thee in the way which thou shalt go. I will guide thee with mine eye. Be ye not as the horse, or as the mule, which have no understanding: whose mouth must be held in with bit and bridle.

God is calling single adults to be guided by the counsel of His eye. He does not want to have to lead you forcibly, as a horse or mule, by bit and bridle.

Do you remember a time as a child when your parents had guests over for dinner? All of you were gathered around the table eating, and someone passed you a plate of snacks. You reached out to grab a fistful—as usual—and all of a sudden you felt your mother glaring at you. She didn't have to say a word. You knew you were out of order. Quickly, your hand shriveled, dropping most of what you had.

What happened? Your mother let you know, with just a look, that you were misbehaving. She guided you with the counsel of her eye.

God wants to be able to do the same thing with you as you walk with Him. He wants you to be so attentive to Him and know Him so well that just the slightest gesture on His part will tell you what He wants from you.

But what happens to many singles is that they get distracted. They're distracted by their desire for marriage. They're distracted by some career objective. They're distracted by this concern, that relationship, or those children, and it forces God to use extraordinary means to get their attention.

Some of these concerns and desires are good ones. There's nothing wrong with desiring a mate, caring for your children, or working well on the job. But when those things take on such astronomic proportions that they crowd out the voice of God in your life, it's time to make some changes.

If God has to knock you down every time He talks to you, doesn't that say something? Doesn't that tell you something is out of whack? Doesn't that tell you that something is wrong in your relationship with Him? What if every time I wanted to get my son's attention, I had to hit him on the head and yell, "Can you hear me?" That wouldn't indicate we had much of a relationship, would it?

But that's the way many singles force God to deal with them. They wait for Him to do something earth-shattering. They wait to hear an audible voice or witness a miracle. They wait to see His word to them skywritten before they respond to His call.

But God doesn't want it that way. He doesn't want to have to take drastic measures. He wants us to be counselled by His eye.

God is looking for single people who are fully attentive to Him, who are waiting upon Him, and who are looking to Him, yielded completely to His will. He's looking for those who are constantly attentive to Him, saying, "Here I am Lord. Send me."

You've got to reach a point in your relationship with God where you are totally attentive to Him and yielded to His purposes. You've got to be so in tune with Him that you know what God wants you to do by His slightest gesture. And you must be ready to do it for

Him, right then and there.

Understand me. I'm not talking about living your life in a super-spiritual, ethereal hover. I don't mean to suggest that you ask God about every minute aspect of your life. For instance, "God, should I brush my teeth this morning?" I'm talking about being committed—heart and soul—to the Lord in a way that can be seen in your attitude and service toward Him. You should know deep in your heart, without reservation, that your life is committed and yielded to the will of God. *Whatever* He wants, you're ready to do it.

That's what Paul is trying to accomplish in 1 Corinthians 7:35. He's trying to develop a people—in this case, single adults—who will give the Lord undistracted devotion.

Let's look at the way some of the other versions translate that verse. The *King James Version* says,

> That ye may *attend* upon the Lord *without* distraction (italics added).

The *Revised Standard Version* says:

> To secure your *undivided* devotion to the Lord (italics added).

The *Phillips Version* says:

> So that your service to God may be, as far as possible, free from worldly distractions.

No matter what version you look at, the message remains the same. God wants you to realize that your singleness is not a disease or a prison to be escaped at all costs. Neither is it an obstacle to be surmounted nor a wall to keep you out of the fullness of life. Your singleness is an opportunity to know Him intimately and to serve Him with your whole heart, soul, mind, and strength.

I believe God wants to develop three qualities in you that will enable you to give Him the absolute dedication He seeks.

The first is the ability to *give God all that you have.* Mark 12:41-44 contains an example of one who did just that:

> And He sat down opposite the treasury, and began observing how the multitude were putting money into the treasury; and many rich people were putting in large sums. And a poor widow came and put in two small copper coins, which amount to a cent. And calling His disciples to Him, He said to them, "Truly I say to you, this poor widow put in more than all the contributors to the treasury; for they all put in out of their surplus, but she, out of her poverty, put in all that she owned, all she had to live on."

Picture yourself among the disciples on that day. You've gone down to the temple with Jesus to watch people put offerings into the treasury. Unlike the quieter collections of today, it's a big show. Donors stroll in, one at a time, dressed in their finest attire. Some even have servants going before them, blowing trumpets to announce their arrival. There's no "don't let your left hand know what your right hand is doing" behavior going on here. The contributors want their audience to know just how much they're willing to give.

One by one they stroll up to the coffer, drag out huge sacks of money, and begin pouring their shiny gold offering into the box. The crowd "oohs" and "ahhs" as the coins pour out, glittering in the sunlight. One offering is bigger than the next.

Then, quietly and unobtrusively, a tiny widow appears on the scene. There is no fanfare for her. In fact, almost no one in the crowd notices her—no one but Jesus. He watches as she pulls two copper coins out of her pocket and drops them into the treasury.

Suddenly, Jesus begins to motion to His disciples. They gather around Him, and He says, "Did you see that offering?" Immediately, they begin mentioning the large sums poured out by bejewelled rabbis in yards of rich clothing. "No, I mean the woman . . . ." The disciples have to think about it for a moment before they recall who she is. "Oh, yes. . .the widow. . . ."

"That woman," Jesus said, "gave more than anyone else."

They can't believe what they're hearing. "What do you mean, she gave more than everyone else? Didn't you see the guy with the bags of gold and the trumpeters?"

Jesus explains: "They all put in out of their surplus, but she, out of her poverty, put in all she owned, all she had to live on."

That single woman, Jesus was saying, gave *all* that she had. She didn't hold back half for herself. She didn't excuse herself, saying, "Well, I'm a little low this week." She took everything she had—every last cent—and gave it to the Kingdom of God.

In the same way, you need to be willing to give God all that you have. You need to be willing to pour out everything, in worship, thanksgiving, and service, to Him.

Now, understand me. I'm not talking about finances alone. I'm talking about giving the Lord everything you are and everything you have. I'm talking about surrendering your possessions, your abilities, your talents, even your desire for relationships, position, and authority to Jesus Christ in total submission. I'm talking about saying, "Lord, here's everything I am—my abilities, my talents, and my skills. Here's everything I own—my car, my home, and my salary. Here's everything I long for—marriage, career, position, authority, and fame. I pour all of it out before You. It's no longer mine. It's Yours. Use it and dispose of it wholly according to Your will."

Sound radical? *It is.* Yet only when you are willing to give everything you are, everything you have, and everything you ever hope to be to the Lord can you truly be undistractedly devoted to Him. Only when you are willing to pour your whole self out as a sacrificial offering to God—to use as He sees fit—will you be able to serve Him without being distracted by other needs, drives, or desires. When you give it all to Him, you'll be able to focus your heart completely upon the Lord and serve Him and Him alone.

Unfortunately, a lot of singles have missed the boat on this issue. They've bought the world's message to them about single living: "You're single. Now's the time to do what you want to do and see what you want to see. You're free. You're free.''

But, for the Christian single, that's not true at all. Your singleness is not your own. It belongs to God because you belong to God.

That means all the freedom you have, all the talents you have, all the abilities you have, and all the time and resources you have are not for spending on yourself. They're for spending on God and on Kingdom purposes. Like no other time in your life, your time as a single person can be poured out fully and completely in service to Him.

What an incredible place you are in, right now. What ability you have as a single adult to be used by Him. You're unencumbered by the restraints brought on by married life. You're free to serve the Lord—wherever and whenever He wants you to. Now *that's* exciting!

But certain liabilities inherent in the single lifestyle itself can present barriers that keep you from realizing this freedom to serve in your day-to-day life. As a single person, your life has an innate tendency to revolve solely around you. Who buys your clothes? Whom do you make dinner for? Whom does your livelihood support? *You.*

Just by its nature, single living is a self-centered lifestyle and, because of that, carries with it the tendency for the single person to become self-involved and depressed. It takes special effort, therefore, for the single person to look beyond himself or herself to others. But it is a necessary thing to do and, the Scriptures say, intrinsic to living a fulfilled life.

Mark 8:35 says,

For whoever wishes to save his life shall

lose it; and whoever loses his life for My
sake and the gospel's shall save it.

Do you want to find life in your singleness? Do you
want to know fulfillment? Then you've got to be willing to make the effort to look beyond yourself to others.
You've got to be willing to give all you have to God.
If you will do that, God promises fulfillment beyond
your wildest dreams.

Matthew 6:33 says,

Seek first His kingdom and His
righteousness; and all these things shall be
added to you.

That's a promise from the Lord himself. God says if
we will seek Him first—before our clothing, before our
job, and before our desire for marriage, career, position, or honor—He will meet the needs of our life and
bless us beyond all that we dare think, ask, or imagine.

Give The Best That You Have

The second quality God wants to develop in you so
you will give Him undistracted devotion is the ability
to *give Him the best that you have*. An example of this
trait can be seen in Mark 14:3-9:

And while He was in Bethany at the home
of Simon the leper, and reclining at the table,
there came a woman with an alabaster vial
of very costly perfume of pure nard; and she
broke the vial and poured it over His head.

But some were indignantly remarking to one another, "Why has this perfume been wasted? For this perfume might have been sold for over three hundred denarii, and the money given to the poor." And they were scolding her. But Jesus said, "Let her alone; why do you bother her? She has done a good deed to Me. For the poor you always have with you, and whenever you wish, you can do them good; but you do not always have Me. She has done what she could; she has anointed My body beforehand for the burial. And truly I say to you, wherever the gospel is preached in the whole world, that also which this woman has done shall be spoken of in memory of her."

Jesus was so satisfied with what this woman did that He said she would be remembered forever for doing it. Wouldn't you like Jesus to be able to say that about you? Wouldn't you like to have your life contribute something that meaningful? But what did she do exactly? Let's take a closer look because I believe you'll find that it's especially significant for you as a single person.

Commentators who've studied this passage in depth say that for a woman of that time period to have such an expensive perfume was rare indeed. They deduce, therefore, that it was most likely her dowry. In Jesus' day, customs required a woman who wanted to get married to present a dowry to the family of her intended spouse. That was the rule. No dowry, no wedding.

But this was not just an anointing, though that, in

itself, was spectacular—a prophetic action, foretelling the suffering of the Savior. It was an act of abandonment, in thanksgiving and love, of the woman's opportunity for marriage before her Lord. In pouring out that precious ointment upon Jesus, she was telling Him: "Lord, I love you. I love you more than anything else in my life, *including* my right to marriage." Jesus knew this and treasured it. He knew she had given Him *the best that she had.*

For many singles, the best they have is their right to marriage. For as long as they can remember, they've dreamt about having a special someone to share their life with. And there's nothing wrong with that desire. God knew it wasn't good for man to be alone and, in the beginning, He created a helpmeet for him. But sometimes that desire for marriage takes on such astronomic proportions that it rivals God for attention. It distracts singles from serving Him with their whole heart.

When I served as an associate pastor of a local church in upstate New York, a young single woman once came to me for counsel. She was depressed and discouraged.She had become interested in a young, single man in the church who didn't even know she was alive. You know the story.

Well, her desire for him grew until she became dominated by her crush. She was gripped by the fantasy of her hoped-for relationship with this fellow. The problem got so severe that it even affected her ability to participate in worship on Sunday. Just one look at this guy would send her into the depths of depression.

Becoming truly upset about what was happening to her, she came to me for advice. Well, I want to be honest with you—I didn't know what to tell her. After listening to her story, I shared some Scripture with her and challenged her to do a few small things. But I didn't feel able to meet her need very well.

A few days later I was walking downtown, and the woman I had counselled came jogging toward me. As I looked into her face, I could see something had changed. Instead of being crestfallen and depressed, a radiance shone about her. Obviously, something dramatic had happened to her. I had to know what had occurred, so I said, "Hey, you look terrific. What happened to you?" Then she told me this story:

> "Yesterday morning, I was taking my usual jog along that big lake just north of the church, and I passed a cemetery. Inside the cemetery stood this huge, rough-hewn cross. I didn't remember having seen it before. All I knew was that something inside of me felt drawn to it.
>
> "On impulse, I ran inside the cemetery gate and began jogging toward the cross. When I got to it, I felt that I should begin digging a hole, right there in front of it. So I did. I clawed away at the grass and began making a hole. Then, again feeling prompted, I took my desire for relationship with that guy in my hands and proceeded to bury it in that hole at the foot of the cross. Then, having covered the hole with dirt and grass, I turned and ran away.
>
> "Mike, ever since that moment I've been a different person. I've been free from that

desire and the discouragement and frustration that went with it. I feel terrific.''

And so did I, just looking at her. In a very graphic way, that woman had been able—literally—to bury her desire for that man at the foot of the cross and be freed to serve the Lord wholly and without distraction.

Perhaps you can relate to this story. You've got a big desire for relationship in your life, and it literally consumes you. Sometimes, especially when you're alone at home on a rainy day, the thoughts of it so devour you that you're left powerless. You feel worthless and empty, too. You've placed your whole heart on that desire for relationship, and, because it isn't there, you feel completely drained.

It's no wonder that, with such a desire gobbling you up inside, you find no joy in your Christian walk. It's no wonder that you find yourself self-centered, weepy, and uncontrollably depressed and negative. You've placed your life and your definition of worth on whether or not you have a special someone in your life, and it's defeating you, wholly and completely.

With your eyes so centered on that desire, there is no way you're going to be able to serve Christ or even get to know Him very well. You're distracted by that desire, and it's robbing you—day after day after day—of joy, fulfillment, power, victory, and purpose.

But you can do something to alleviate the problem. You can take that desire and do what that single lady did. Bury it at the foot of the cross—not literally, necessarily, but at least in your heart. You can let go of the desire that's controlling your life. You can let go of your dream and give it to the Lord.

Please understand me. I am not saying you should take a pledge to stay single forever. Neither am I saying you shouldn't have a desire to be married. But you must keep marriage in proper perspective—that is, under the Lordship of Jesus Christ.

When the best dreams of your heart—be they for marriage, children, career, home, or family—are poured out before the Lord and relinquished to His Lordship, then you will be able to seek Him first and give Him your undivided attention.

Do What You Can Do

The third quality God wants to develop in you so that you may give Him undistracted devotion is the ability to *do what you can do*.

The woman who anointed Jesus' feet practiced this quality. She took the oil that she had and poured it out before the Lord.

I'm sure she thought that anointing Jesus with oil was an insignificant gesture on her part. I'm sure she wasn't aware of the spiritual implications of the act. So, compared to the disciples, who were leaving behind homes, families, and jobs to follow Christ, her task was fairly simple. Oh, she gave the best that she had. We know that, and she knew that. But, compared to what others were doing, it didn't look like much.

She could have been discouraged as she poured out that ointment. She could have looked at what she was doing and thought, Gee, this is such a little thing to do for One who means so much to me. And she could have allowed that thought to keep her from doing it. But because she didn't, because she did what she could do, she ended up being used in prophetic ministry before the Lord. And Jesus said that wherever the Gospel was preached, she would be spoken of and remembered for what she had done.

As a single person, it's not uncommon for you to wonder whether your life will touch another's with significance. This thought comes into your head as a by-product of single living as a whole. You come home every night, many times to an empty apartment, perhaps miles away from relatives and close friends. And you wonder, If I died tonight, would anybody notice? Would anybody care? Or would my body just lie here for days before anyone came to find me?

I know singles who think that way. They're sure they're insignificant. They're sure they're so little needed by others that they could indeed die tomorrow without notice. Now, that may not be the case, but when you come home night after night to an empty apartment, you can begin to feel that way.

Closely related to that discouraging thought is the longing to make a difference in the world around you, to count for something in someone else's life, and to be remembered. The woman in this Bible passage was. Why? Because she was willing to do what she could do.

Many singles look at their lives and get caught up in the things they cannot do. "I can't sing like so and so. I can't preach like so and so. I can't build things like so and so," they say. But in thinking that way, they discourage themselves from taking *any* action whatsoever and keep themselves from experiencing the fulfillment that could be theirs by doing what they could do.

God is not interested in having you tackle some mammoth task beyond your ability. He's not interested in having you sing like Cathy, type like Elaine, or organize big events like Jim. He's only interested in having you do what you can do.

If you're a typist, God wants you to use that skill to serve Him. If you're a waitress, God wants you to serve as though you were waiting on Him. If you're a mechanic, He wants you to work as if it were His car you were servicing. If you're a businessman, God wants you to deal honestly, in a Christian manner, doing everything as unto Him. If you're gifted in music, writing, art, or dance, don't bury it. Use it for the glory of God. Do what *you* can do.

"But Mike, all I can do is set up chairs on Sundays. All I can do is usher. All I can do is greet people at the door." Great! Go ahead and do it. It doesn't matter what you do, as long as you do what you can. That's all God is looking for.

In Matthew 25:14-29, we read a parable about three servants, each of whom were called to do what they could do:

> For it is just like a man about to go on a journey, who called his own slaves, and entrusted his possessions to them. And to one he gave five talents, to another, two, and to another, one, each according to his ability; and he went on his journey. Immediately the one who had received the five talents went and traded with them, and gained five more talents. In the same manner the one who had received the two talents gained two more. But he who received the one talent

went away and dug in the ground, and hid his master's money.

Now after a long time the master of those slaves came and settled accounts with them. And the one who had received the five talents came up and brought five more talents, saying, "Master, you entrusted five talents to me; see, I have gained five more talents." His master said to him, "Well done, good and faithful slave; you were faithful with a few things, I will put you in charge of many things, enter into the joy of your master." The one also who had received the two talents came up and said, "Master, you entrusted to me two talents; see, I have gained two more talents." His master said to him, "Well done, good and faithful slave; you were faithful with a few things, I will put you in charge of many things; enter into the joy of your master." And the one also who had received the one talent came up and said, "Master, I knew you to be a hard man, reaping where you did not sow, and gathering where you scattered no seed. And I was afraid, and went away and hid your talent in the ground; see, you have what is yours." But his master answered and said to him, "You wicked, lazy slave, you knew that I reap where I did not sow, and gather where I scattered no seed. Then you ought to have put my money in the bank, and on my arrival I would have received my money back with interest. Therefore take away the talent from him, And give it to the one who has the ten talents.'' For to everyone who has shall more be given, and he shall have an abundance; but from the one who does not have, even what he does have shall be taken away.

Here we have three men. Each has been entrusted with a certain number of talents—one with five, another with two, and a third with one, each according to his ability.

I want you to recognize something right from the start: each person had a purpose. There wasn't one person the master overlooked. He didn't do what you or I might have. He didn't look at the capacity of the five-talent man and entrust his whole fortune to him, leaving the other two men to tag along, helping him out. He looked at their abilities and gave them each a purpose in keeping with their potential. Then he went away, trusting them to use their talents wisely.

When he returned, he found that both the five-talent man and the two-talent man had used what was given to them prudently and had managed to double it for the master. But the one-talent man, being fearful, had buried his talent in the ground, doing nothing with it until the master returned. The master was exceedingly pleased over the work of the first two. They had been good stewards of their talents. But he rebuked the third man and called him wicked and lazy.

It's important to note that the reward had nothing to do with the amount produced. It had to do with the degree of faithfulness in the servant to do what he could do. The five-talent man used his talents and doubled them. So did the two-talent man. Both used what they had to the fullest. But the one-talent man looked at what he had and buried it instead of using it to its full advantage.

Let's take a closer look. The five-talent man was the type of person you knew in school who could do everything well—he was quarterback on the high school varsity team, leading man in the school play, and the tops academically in his class.

But the two-talent man and the one-talent man were, more or less, equals. The two-talent had several fine abilities. He was skilled in a few areas. The one-talent man also had ability—he was especially gifted in one particular way. Yet the way these two responded to the master differed drastically. One did what he could with what he had. The other buried it and got chided for it.

What made the one-talent man bury his talent? From looking at my life and this passage of Scripture, I come up with several reasons. For one thing, he compared his abilities with that of the other two men. "That five-talent guy has so much ability. He could do a lot more than I could ever do—without even trying. That two-talent man has twice as much ability as I do. He'll do better than I for sure. The best I could do would be pitiful compared to them, so I might as well just quit right now."

Secondly, we see the master call the one-talent man "wicked" and "lazy." Could it be that the one-talent man only used comparison as an excuse for laziness? How many times have you done that—used "I can't do this" or "I can't do that" as an excuse for personal laziness? You really don't *want* to reach. You really don't *want* to stretch. You really don't *want* to try.

You'd rather stay where you are than go through the struggle that growing and giving one hundred percent entails. This passage indicates that an element of laziness quenched the one-talent man's motivation.

Thirdly, the man may have chosen to bury his talent because he feared failure. "What if I try and I fail? What if I do something and it doesn't measure up? I might as well bury it. If I do that, at least I can't lose it. If I put it in the ground, at least it won't get taken." He wasn't willing to risk.

Finally, this man misunderstood the master. He thought he would be judged for how much he accomplished rather than for what he did with what he had.

Many singles suffer with the same problems that this one-talent man had. First, they compare themselves, ability for ability, with others. "I can't sing like Joanie. I can't play guitar like Sam. I can't speak in front of people like Max. I can't do street witnessing like Jamie." And they disqualify themselves from service.

Sometimes they're also lazy, making excuses for not serving God. "I'm not married yet. I'm too young. I'm too old. I'm a new Christian. I've been wounded by divorce. I'm a single parent—I've got children to attend to." While some of these may be true and valid and have their root in real areas of responsibility, there's a line over which you cross that becomes a wall erected to keep yourself from serving God. You've got a "good" excuse.

Many singles also become plagued by fear of failure. Many have seen important relationships collapse before their eyes, despite all their attempts to restore it. Others have tried and failed at work. It's left them bruised and empty inside, fearful of trying—and failing —all over again. So they adopt a "no-risk" mentality. "If I don't try, at least I'll never be disappointed. If I don't try, at least I won't fail." But thinking like that only keeps them from growing in Christ and doing what God calls them to do.

Listen to me. God is not concerned about what Jamie can do—or Bobby, Sally, or Sue—that's "better" than what you can do. He's only concerned with having *you* do what *you can do.* If that's setting up chairs on Sunday, fine. If it's typing letters for the pastor, great. If it's balancing the accounts in a bank or other business, terrific. If it's singing, playing an instrument, or speaking, wonderful. *Whatever* you can do, God wants you to do that.

He doesn't have any expectations of you that exceed the abilities you have. He knows what you can accomplish—and what you can't. He knows what abilities He's given to you, and He doesn't expect more from you than that.

But He does expect you to do what you can do. He does expect you to use the talents, abilities, and skills you *do* have—be they natural or instilled by the power of God—for His glory.

God doesn't look at the magnitude of the gift. He looks at the giver's ability to give. He doesn't look at the size of an offering but the amount left in a person's pocket. He doesn't look at how much ministry a person does, only how much is held back. God is not concerned with how much you do but that you do what you can with what you have.

So there they are: three qualities that will enable you to give God undistracted devotion.

One: Give all that you have. Surrender every desire, every thought, every ability, and every personality trait to the Lordship of Jesus Christ and allow Him to use them as He sees fit.

Two: Give the best that you have. Be willing to surrender that supreme desire—be it for marriage, a career objective, or a lifestyle—to Him to dispose of or reclaim wholly according to His will. Make Him your supreme desire.

Three: Do what you can do. Take the talents, abilities, and skills God has bestowed upon you and use them for His glory.

If you will, by the grace and transforming power of God, be faithful to do these things, you'll find yourself undistractedly devoted to Him and reap the benefits besides: a whole, complete, satisfying, purpose-filled life in Christ.

Chapter Five

DISCOVER YOUR PURPOSE

Your singleness provides you with a special opportunity to discover your purpose in Christ.

That's right. Your singleness need not be merely a waiting period in which you wait for life to begin. It can and should be a time to serve the Lord fully in the purpose He has created just for you.

God has a special plan for your life that doesn't have to wait for marriage in order to be fulfilled. It's a purpose He's created just for you, for which He has equipped you and you alone.

How do you know what God's specific purpose is for you? I believe it can be found, first of all, in the fabric of your own being—the blueprint God created for you while you were yet in your mother's womb. Jeremiah 1:5 says,

> Before I formed you in the womb I knew you, and before you were born I consecrated you; I have appointed you a prophet to the nations.

Isn't that a staggering thought? Before Jeremiah was ever born, God knew him and had a plan for his life. Just as surely, God has known you and has a plan for you. Psalm 139:13-16 says

> For Thou didst form my inward parts;
> Thou didst weave me in my mother's womb.
> I will give thanks to Thee, for I am fearfully and wonderfully made; wonderful are Thy works, and my soul knows it very well. My frame was not hidden from Thee, when I was made in secret, and skillfully wrought in the depths of the earth.
> Thine eyes have seen my unformed substance; and in Thy book they were all written, the days that were ordained for me, when as yet there were none of them.

Here, again, we realize that God has been involved with our life since before we were born. Before our mothers even sensed our presence, God knew us. More than that, He was actively involved in our formation—in the features and the coloring we would have, the talents and skills we would possess, and the temperament through which He would display His glory. He planned it all so that one day we would glorify Him in a particular way.

That means *nothing* inside of us is an accident. Our skills, our talents, our looks, and our abilities—everything we are—were put in us for a purpose: that we may fulfill *His* purpose for our lives.

That means we can look at who we are humanly and

get a fairly good indication of the person God has called us to be. If we're talented in art, God wants to use us in that way. If math is our strong suit, God wants to use that ability to glorify Himself. If we enjoy serving others as a hostess, waitress, hotel person, homemaker, child care worker, or flight attendant, that is no accident, either. God has put a heart in us for that kind of work, and He wants to glorify Himself through us. If you're a mechanic, a body worker, an engineer, a bus driver, a conductor, a warehouse worker, or a salesman, God wants to use you for His glory. There's no limit to what He can do. All you need to do is be aware of the talents He's given you and use them.

You can look, too, at your family background, your home life, your education, your training, your religious affiliation, and your social interests to find still more clues. Oh, your background may be filled with all sorts of non-God-glorifying events. Your parents may have been divorced, or you may have been an orphan. You may have had a very secular upbringing, where God was never mentioned. Maybe you had a bad period of rebellion—taking drugs, drinking, participating in immoral activities, even disdaining those who believed in God and chiding them right to their face. That certainly wasn't God's will for your life. But today, as a Christian, you can take a new look at the fabric of your life and allow God to weave it into the marvelous plan He has prepared especially for you.

Romans 8:28 says,

> And we know that God causes all things to work together for good to those who love God, to those who are called according to His purpose.

Today, as a Christian single, you love God and have been called according to His purpose. Therefore, God wants to use everything you are, everything you can do, and everything you've ever been through to bring Him glory and honor and produce fruits of righteousness in the earth.

You can look at your environment—and your response to it—and see there a reflection of what God has called you to be in His Kingdom. What did you enjoy doing in school? What things inspired you? What kind of experiences made you want to excel? What was your home life like? What kind of religious upbringing did you have? What extracurricular activities did you enjoy? All these things can provide clues to the purpose God has for your life.

"But, Mike, what if I look at myself and don't see anything particularly outstanding about me? What if I see a minus 35?"

Well, I know just how you feel, believe me. All I need to do is take one look at my own life to know that nothing in it recommended me for service. A shy, gawky, over-sensitive kid, I was average in school. I got mostly *Cs*. As far as home life goes, mine wasn't exactly the best. I grew up in a single-parent household. My church background was minimal, and I had no real relationship with God—just an outer coating of religious training.

When I looked at my life, I didn't see much God could use. But God spoke to me, as He did to Jeremiah, and told me—a shy, nervous kid—that I, of all people, was going to be "a prophet to the nations." More than that, He took me, a married person, and gave me a ministry to singles. Isn't that unbelievable? Yes, it really is. Yet God has moved in my life, equipped me for the ministry He's called me to, and caused the impossible to happen.

How did it get accomplished? By His grace. You can look at your life and not see much to recommend you for service. But that doesn't matter in the Kingdom of God. What God calls you to do, He equips you for—by natural abilities, yes, but also, and most importantly, by His grace.

It doesn't matter if you have only a limited education, lack a skill in sports, have physical disabilities, are shy or nervous, are old or young, or lack any other thing you think is necessary for service. God can and will use you. He will enable you *by His grace*.

I once taught a class at a Bible school, and I met a young woman who had cerebral palsy. Her body was crippled but not her attitude about life. She wrote a story about living with her handicap. I'd like to share it with you.

What's It Like?

"What's it like being handicapped? Well, it's hard for the handicapped to accept what they have. Other people make fun of them. Some people who have handicaps give up. They think they can't do things. They can if they try.

"I'm handicapped. I have cerebral palsy. I wanted to give up, but I didn't. I went on. Also, I'm a Christian, and that means I belong to Jesus forever and ever. My handicaps belong to Him now.

"I'd like to tell you a story that happened to me. My

doctor told me that I wouldn't be able to play the piano because I didn't have enough strength in my fingers. I took piano lessons for four years. I didn't give up, but I went on. I play hymns and Christian music all the time. And when I play them, they are prayers to Jesus.

"People think I can't do things because of my handicaps. But I go roller skating, drive a car, love to sing, and many more things. These are gifts that God has given to me.

"Look at Joni Eareckson. She's in a wheelchair, and she didn't give up. She went on like me. Even though she's paralyzed from the neck down, she can drive a van. Joni loves the Lord and travels all over the world and preaches.

"Sometimes people feel sorry for us. We don't need that at all. God has a plan for me, and I must be patient and be ready to do His will. 'I can do all things through Christ who strengthens me' (Philippians 4:13)."

This young woman could have chosen to be discouraged and defeated in life. Instead, she saw her potential in Christ and was able to believe Him for great things. Humanly speaking, many limitations were placed on this girl's life. But, by God's grace, she remained optimistic and believed He would use her for great exploits in His Kingdom.

The more reasons you can list why God shouldn't use you, the more He sees you as a prime candidate for service. 2 Corinthians 4:7 says,

> But we have this treasure in earthen
> vessels, that the surpassing greatness of the

power may be of God and not from ourselves.

Have you ever gone into a greenhouse and seen a beautiful plant inside a rather homely pot—the plant is gorgeous, but the pot you could do without? That's the way God likes to be inside us. He likes to be the beautiful plant inside your ordinary clay pot. When He is, people get caught up with Him rather than you, and that's His objective. He wants to get the glory.

The more you look at yourself and see what disqualifies you for service, the more God wants to use you. When He uses you, everyone will know that it's God.

1 Corinthians 1:26-29 says,

> For consider your calling, brethren, that there were not many wise according to the flesh, not many mighty, not many noble; but God has chosen the foolish things of the world to shame the wise, and God has chosen the weak things of the world to shame the things which are strong, and the base things of the world and the despised, God has chosen, the things that are not, that He might nullify the things that are, that no man should boast before God.

Do you look at your life and see weakness? Do you feel despised, rejected, and worthless? Do you feel too old, too young, or too unable? Great! God wants to use you. In fact, you're the very person He's looking for. In you, He can really shine.

The apostle Paul grasped this idea readily and rejoiced:

> Most gladly, therefore, I will rather boast about my weaknesses, that the power of Christ may dwell in me. Therefore I am well content with weaknesses, with insults, with distresses, with persecutions, with difficulties, for Christ's sake; for when I am weak, then I am strong (2 Corinthians 12:9-10).

If you look at your life—that marriage that ended in divorce, that body depleted with age, that much-scarred ego wounded by rejection—and think God can't use you, I want you to know you're wrong. He not only can but He wants to, even more than you want to be used by Him. You were created for a purpose, and, despite all the things you see that make you sure you can't be used by God, He will see that purpose fulfilled.

God will take any painful experience of singleness and use it for His glory. But you must take who you are and what you've experienced—both the bad and the good—and offer it to Him. Today, if you will yield every talent, every ability, every fault, every weakness, and every wound to the Lord, He will begin to use those things to bear everlasting fruit in His Kingdom.

The Importance Of Vision

God does not want us wandering aimlessly, yielding ourselves to every cause that comes along. He wants us channelled into a specific realm of service. To do that, we need a sense of *personal vision*. Personal vision gives us a long-range objective to shoot for that keeps us "in line" in the here and now. Personal vision gives us a view of where and how God wants us to serve Him ultimately that affects the way we live today.

A sense of personal vision gives scope and dimension to our lives, parameters within which we operate today to help fulfill God's ultimate will for our lives. Without this sense of vision, a person will have a tendency to drift, and their resistance to temptation will be low.

Proverbs 29:18 says,

> Where there is no vision, the people are unrestrained.

People without vision live careless lives. Undirected by an ultimate objective, they have a tendency to wander off course, to waste time, and to lose conviction and motivation. They live day to day without any sense of the future, and it causes them to refrain from disciplines that could prepare them for it.

Most of us have experienced "the blues" that come in early spring when we realize we've gotten just a bit too chubby to climb into our summer clothing. All winter long we sat in front of the TV set, shoveling food into our mouths and gaining weight.

While the snow flew, we hardly gave a thought to summer—at least not one that caused us to change the way we were taking care of ourselves during the cold winter months. Then spring came, along with thoughts of the beach and swimming. Immediately, we saw ourselves sunning amid a wash of humanity. No way am I putting a body like this on the beach, we thought. And we began a mad rush of diet and exercise meant to get us slim and trim for summer.

All winter long we lived careless lives, without vision, and it caused us to become physically lazy and indulgent. Then, with the first twinge of spring, we got a vision of summer, and it inspired us to exercise discipline in diet and exercise so we might be ready to face the summer when it came.

A personal vision does the same thing for us spiritually. It gives us a vision of who God has called us to be and influences the way we live today.

How can you receive a personal vision for your life? There are a number of ways.

The first way is through the Word of God itself. You will be reading the Word, when suddenly a verse seems to come alive for you personally. God is speaking especially to you in that moment, and He gives you a vision for your life.

A second way vision is revealed is through Christian books. You could be reading a biography, for example, of a great man or woman of God and begin to identify with their calling, their struggles, their beliefs, and their life. In that instance, God may be tugging on your heart, directing you to or confirming a path He has chosen for your life.

A third way vision is revealed is through the confirming word of another person.

I remember a time during Bible school when the vice president of the school did that for me. A group of my classmates and I were gathered at his home for fellowship and discussion, when all at once he turned to me and, with a perfect Welsh accent, said, "Mike, what do you want to do with your life?"

Now Brother David Edwards was an astute man, so discerning, I thought, that he knew everything that ever went through my head. I was sure that even my most innocent statement could reveal more of me to him than I wanted him to know. That made me a little nervous whenever I spoke to him.

So, when he asked me this question, I wanted my answer to be good. I wanted him to be impressed. I shifted in my seat just slightly, then replied, "I want to do whatever God wants me to do, Brother Edwards. If God wants me to pump gas, I'll pump gas. If He wants me to sell insurance, I'll sell insurance. I'll do *anything* He wants me to do."

That's a spiritual answer, isn't it? It sounds good, doesn't it? But to Brother Edwards it just didn't ring true. He leaned forward in his seat, drawing his face closer to mine. "Mike, what do *you* really want to do?" I thought again. I wanted to be honest, now—as honest as I possibly could be. Then I said, in a moment of boldness, "I want to be the best preacher I can be."

Brother Edwards, who is now president of that Bible school, was and is one of the most eloquent speakers I had ever heard. When he spoke in class or in chapel, his words carried with them the power and authority of God. So, saying I wanted to be the best preacher was a gutsy thing to do. I felt sure he would reprimand me or at least chide me for being so presumptuous.

But he didn't. Instead, he looked at me and said, "Well, why don't you go ahead and do it, then?" His words sunk deep into my spirit. Yeah, I thought, why don't I? And in that moment, with those few words, Brother Edwards released me to follow God's will for my life.

Setting Realistic Goals

Nothing is wrong with pumping gas, selling insurance, or any other thing God may want you to do. It's just not what the Lord was calling me to do. It wasn't what He had equipped me for.

Inside of you is something you, personally, have been equipped by God to do. Perhaps you've been called to be a teacher, an administrator, a business executive, a secretary, a waitress, a construction worker, a bookstore owner, a cook, or a mechanic. God has placed *that* purpose on your heart, and you want to fulfill it.

Well, chances are you're not that person now. That's just a vision God has given you. How do you go about progressing toward that vision? *By setting goals that you can accomplish now.*

What are goals? Goals are measurable purposes that enable us to walk, step by step, toward the vision God has for our lives. Let me give you some examples.

To be a great mountain climber is a vision; to climb Pike's Peak in January is a goal.

To reach a neighbor for Christ is a vision; to have a Bible study in my home on December 10 and invite my neighbors is a goal.

Goals give us concrete ways to develop into the person God has called us to be and the purpose He has set aside especially for us. They also give us a tangible way of measuring how far along we've come in that vision.

When God told me I was going to be "a prophet to the nations," I was nowhere near fulfillment of that calling. Inside, I still had a lot of growing to do.

But I earnestly desired to pursue God's call on my life and to "go ahead and do it," as Brother Edwards had said. So I began doing what I could do. I called up the pastors of several local churches and asked if I could speak to their congregations. They refused. I was still so young and untried. What could I do?

Well, the school I went to had something called an "outstation" program. The purpose of the program was to give students practical experience in ministry, in addition to their study time, while also helping local ministers with the work they needed to do.

One of the outstations served the downtown mission. There, street people could get a hot meal if they were willing to listen to someone preach for half an hour. "Would they let me preach?" I asked the person in charge of the outstation. "Sure," he told me, and that's how I began my preaching ministry—talking to a group of destitute men at an inner-city mission.

That doesn't sound much like a "prophet to the nations," does it? And I wasn't. Not yet. But I was growing, step by step, into that vision by accomplishing goals that were presently within my reach.

The same thing will be true for you. God may call you to be president of IBM, and that's great. But it isn't going to happen right away. You're going to be groomed for it first. Setting and achieving goals that you're able to accomplish *now* is the way that happens.

Goals are also *faith achievements,* in which we reach out in faith and lay hold of the future. Right now, as founder and director of a nationwide single adult ministry, I'm reaching out and laying hold of the year ahead. I'm planning all our activities for next year in faith.

For you, it may not be as far reaching. Perhaps it will only be a few months down the line, or less. But you *should* be reaching into the future and taking it by faith.

Get out there and volunteer to help the handicapped if you're called to the health care field. If education is your sphere, assist a local teacher in grading papers or tutoring students. Get out and help the local Right-to-Life group if law or social action is your calling. Assist a Christian counsellor in their work if that's the area where God wants you to work.

There are thousands of ways to begin—thousands of places aching for dedicated people with a sense of vision and commitment to work with them. Go to your pastor if you need help finding a place to serve. Perhaps even advertise your availability in your church bulletin. Chances are a member of your church is involved or burdened with the same calling or knows someone who is. Take the first step. Get involved.

And, above all, don't let fear or worry stop you. I know a lot of singles who won't set goals for themselves because they're afraid of failure. But it's impossible to fail totally if you dare to try. *Success involves risk*. And, in the Christian life, it's not risking by yourself but with God at your side. As Paul says, "If God is for us, who is against us?" (Romans 8:31).

Not too long ago, I spoke at the Christ For The Nations Institute in Dallas, Texas. I stayed for a week, speaking each morning in their chapel service. After each session, the students would line up to talk to me at the speaker's platform, which stood a few steps up from the floor.

One day as we were chatting, I looked out into the auditorium and saw a little man in a wheelchair rolling toward the platform. He was a small, frail man—his legs just managed to reach out over the edge of his seat.

I watched as this man got a few of the students to help him up to the platform, where he got in line with the others. Finally, his turn came to speak to me. I bowed down to say hello, and he grabbed my hand. His eyes met mine, and without another word he began to speak:

> Far better it is to dare mighty things, win glorious triumphs, even though checkered by failure, than to take rank with those poor spirits who neither enjoy much nor suffer much because they live in the gray twilight that knows not victory nor defeat.

The words were F.D. Roosevelt's, but it was obvious they held special meaning to this handicapped gentleman. "Mike," he said, still looking at me, "I *know* God is going to do something with my life." The man spoke with conviction. I knew that, despite all his physical disabilities, this man had a sense of personal vision. He was a person of destiny.

You, too, are a person of destiny. From before you were born, God had a plan for your life. That plan cannot be thwarted by any disability you have—physical, relational, or otherwise. No matter what you've been through, God can still use you. No matter how wounded you are, how powerless you feel, or how untalented and unskilled you perceive yourself to be, God has a plan for your life, and He is big enough to see that plan fulfilled in you today.

The only thing that can keep you from being what God wants you to be is an act of your will. You *can* choose to let the limitations you see keep you from experiencing fullness in Jesus Christ. You can allow the rejections and hurts of the past to bind you to a lonely, purposeless life. You can allow fear to hem you in on all sides and freeze you up so you never go anywhere in God.

Or you can take all that you are—both in weakness and in strength—pour it out before the Lord, and experience healing, power, fulfillment, and usefulness in the Kingdom of God.

God wants you to be fulfilled, and He wants you to have purpose and meaning. He wants you to be healed and freed of the hurt, rejection, and fears that have bound you. And He's provided a way through Jesus Christ, His Son.

If you will begin to trust Jesus today—lay all your burdens upon Him—and in faith begin to walk in the purpose He has laid upon your heart, you will begin to know joy, meaning, purpose, and wholeness. You'll discover that true fulfillment is not in any human relationship, no matter how deep, but in an ever-deepening relationship with Jesus Christ.

You possess within you the talent and ability to be used greatly in the Kingdom of God. You possess the gifts and the skills needed to do what He has called you to do. And, most importantly, you possess His Holy Spirit—the Enabler and Empowerer—Who will protect, guide, strengthen, and embolden you to do what God has called you to do. Trust in Him today, and begin living the life God has destined especially for you.

Faithful is He who calls you, and He also
will bring it to pass (1 Thessalonians 5:24).

Chapter Six

THE ARMY OF GOD

You are part of a mighty army God is raising up to spearhead the greatest revival the world has ever seen.

When I first got involved in singles ministry, I wondered why. What was I doing here in the first place? I knew that many people were single today because of the breakdown of the family. Divorce, immorality, and unfaithfulness were destroying more men and women than ever before. I also knew Satan was at the root of this destruction. So I wondered: Why would God want me involved in something that was so obviously the work of Satan? Shouldn't I be doing something to build up families instead? Shouldn't I be doing something to reclaim what was lost through Satan's deceptions and destructive measures?

As I pondered this, the Lord reminded me of the story of Joseph. Here was a young man to whom God had given a vision of great leadership but who, along the way, seemed to suffer only hardship.

Later, when Joseph became a leader in Pharaoh's court, a famine struck the land, and many people came to him for aid. His brothers, who had treated him so harshly before, were among them.

At first, the brothers didn't know who he was. Then Joseph revealed himself to them. Immediately, they became afraid. Would the brother they had so hatefully abused now turn on them in vengeance?

We know from the account in Genesis that he didn't. Instead, he forgave them and gave them a share in the abundance of material wealth that God had given him. But the brothers continued to fear his retaliation and, even when Joseph was near death, remained afraid.

Just a few days before he died, Joseph made a final attempt to lay those fears to rest and tried to reassure them with these words:

> You intended to harm me, but God intended it for good to accomplish what is now being done, the saving of many lives. So then, don't be afraid. I will provide for you and your children (Genesis 50:20-21 NIV).

The words, "You intended to harm me, but God intended it for good" reverberated in my mind. I read it again. Then the Lord began to speak: "Satan meant it for evil, but I meant it for good."

In a flash I understood why God wanted me involved with single adults. Though Satan had indeed dealt destructively with families, God had it in mind to use that thing for good. He wanted to use those people—always single, widowed, and divorced—for His glory. He wanted to redeem them and use them to produce a bountiful harvest for His Kingdom.

Suddenly, in my mind, I saw before me a vast field

of single adults, an army of believers capable of wholehearted, undistracted devotion to Him. Empowered and sent forth by God's Spirit, they were capable of spearheading the greatest revival the world had ever known.

You, as a single adult, are a part of that mighty plan. You are a special tool in the hand of God, a finely crafted instrument who, mobilized by His Spirit, is capable of doing great things for the furtherance of His Kingdom.

Unlike a teenager or a college student, you are trained and experienced in a particular field. You have talents and abilities honed over many years. You are not a person on your way to becoming a doctor, nurse, teacher, business manager, secretary, mechanic, or home manager. You are *already* established, actively practicing in an area of expertise. Just imagine what God could do with a person like you—and there are thousands of single adults in the world today—if you took hold of Paul's challenge and gave yourself wholly unto the Lord.

David's mighty men were people like that. 1 Chronicles 12:38 describes them, saying,

> All these, being men of war, who could draw up in battle formation, came to Hebron with a perfect heart to make David king over all Israel; and all the rest also of Israel were of one mind to make David king.

Today, when we read the word "perfect" we think of something without flaw. But that's not the way the writer of Chronicles meant it. When he used the word, it meant "whole" or "complete." David's mighty men were wholehearted men. They were completely committed to David, with no reservations. And because of this unwavering devotion, there was nothing they couldn't do. Because there was nothing else vying for their affections, they were able to give themselves completely to the task set before them and conquer even their greatest enemies in the name of their God.

I believe God is grooming you—even now—for a place in His army. I believe He is calling you to become wholeheartedly devoted to Him—to leave all distractions behind and serve Him one hundred percent.

Why? Because it's only the person who has left all else behind—who has said "God, you mean more to me that the home I've lived in for years, the people I've come to know and love, and the plans I've made for my career and my personal life'—who can truly serve the Lord with all their heart. If there is anything else on the back burner of their heart, it will sap strength from their commitment to God and may cause them, ultimately, to wander away from serving Him. It may even cause them to backslide.

Remember the girl I talked to you about back in the second chapter? That was her problem. She desired marriage more than Jesus Christ. And, even though she was bearing much fruit in ministry, she gave it all up when the opportunity to fulfill that desire came up.

God doesn't want that to happen to you. That's why He's so concerned about developing an undivided heart in you. He wants you to be completely free to serve Him—and not be in danger of losing relationship with Him altogether.

God is calling you to be a member of His army and

to serve Him with an undivided heart. And, in order to bring you to that place, He's allowing you to go through all kinds of struggles in your walk with Him.

Whether you're struggling with low self-esteem or the pain of past abuses, with raising your children alone or dealing with the death of your spouse, with getting along with others in your church or doing a good job at work, God is trying to do something in your life. He's trying to train you for service in His army—the army of God.

God wants to use your abilities, talents, skills, and experience to change the world. He wants you to pour out everything you have before Him in service. Whether you're a secretary, a businessman, a carpenter, an advertising executive, or a homemaker, God wants to use you. He has a place for you in His army.

In a familiar passage of 1 Corinthians 12, Paul says:

> For the body is not one member, but many. If the foot should say, "Because I am not a hand, I am not a part of the body," it is not for this reason any the less a part of the body. And if the ear should say, "Because I am not an eye, I am not a part of the body," it is not for this reason any the less a part of the body. If the whole body were an eye, where would the hearing be? If the whole were hearing, where would the sense of smell be? But now God has placed the members, each one of them, in the body, just as He desired (verses 14-18).

You have been given abilities, just as God desired.

You have been equipped for a purpose. If your skill is typing, then you should type. If you can carry a tune, then sing. If you're mechanically inclined, then serve the Lord and the Body with your skills. If you've got the gift of leadership, then use it to the glory of God.

You are part of the army of God, which is moving out to transform the world. You are part of a mighty movement that will not—and cannot—be quenched.

God is calling forth His mighty army, a battalion of highly motivated single adults devoted to serving Him. He is looking for those who are willing to give all they have, the best they have, and whatever they have for His Kingdom and His purposes. He is calling you today. Will you answer the call to service? Will you give Him one hundred percent? Or will you put down this book and walk away? The choice is yours.

* * * * * * * * * * * *

Throughout this book I have shared with you the principles that will release you for wholehearted service to God. Only in centering your life upon Jesus Christ and finding your fulfillment in Him will you find release. Surrendering all that you have and the best that you have to Him will free you to give Him undistracted devotion. I have told you that it is in doing what you can do that you will find the meaning you seek. And I have told you that God's purpose for your life can be found within the person He has created you to be.

But the future lies in your hands. It is you who will choose how you respond to your singleness. It is you who will choose whether you live your life in a holding pattern, waiting for that special someone to come along, or live for the most special Someone, Jesus Christ. You will decide which you love best—some object or desire or Jesus Christ. It is you, and you alone, who will determine the outcome.

God has provided a way out of your loneliness. He has provided a way for you to be fulfilled and complete. God has designed a special purpose for you that you can begin fulfilling right now.

But He cannot force it upon you. Nor does He want to. He gave you a free will to choose Him or not to choose Him—to choose His way or your own. That is as viable today as before you accepted Christ. You can choose.

Remember what Jesus said: He who saves his life will lose it, but he who loses his life for My sake and the Gospel's shall keep it to life eternal. (See Matthew 16:25; Mark 8:35; Luke 9:24.)

Your singleness can be an experience frustrated by unfulfilled dreams, shattered hopes, vain imaginings, discouragement, doubt, and fear. Or, received as the opportunity for service that it is, it can become a fertile valley of completion, joy, purpose, godly ambition, and fruitfulness. It is your choice. Choose today whom you will serve.

About the Author

A motivating speaker in great demand, Mike Cavanaugh travels extensively, challenging thousands to total commitment to Jesus Christ.

The instructor of evangelism at Elim Bible Institute in Lima, New York, he is founder and executive director of B.A.S.I.C. (Brothers and Sisters in Christ), a local church-based college ministry, and Mobilized To Serve (M.T.S.), a nationwide single adult ministry. Both B.A.S.I.C. and M.T.S. are transdenominational ministries sponsored by Elim Fellowship.

B.A.S.I.C. was established in 1980 to aid local churches in reaching out to college campuses in their area. The ministry currently serves students on twenty-five campuses.

Mobilized To Serve (M.T.S.) was formed in August, 1981, to "equip and mobilize singles for service in the Body of Christ." Since then, more than fifty thousand single adults in both the United States and Canada—including the divorced, the widowed, and single parents—have attended its conferences and singles days and received teaching through an active audio and video tape ministry. The ministry also publishes a quarterly periodical for singles, called *Single Impact*.

A frequent guest lecturer at Christ For The Nations Institute, Mike has appeared on the *700 Club* and the

Trinity Broadcasting Network, and has spoken at many nationwide rallies, including the *Creation* and *Fishnet* festivals.

Mike is 32 years old and has been married to his wife, Terri, for ten years. They have two children.

SINGLE IMPACT

A Magazine Equipping Single Adults
To Make an Eternal Difference in Their World

If you've enjoyed the teaching you've received through Mike's book and you'd like to hear more, there's a way you can do just that—through a FREE SUBSCRIPTION to *Single Impact,* Mike Cavanaugh's quarterly magazine for single adults. Geared to equip singles to serve the Lord with their whole hearts and make an eternal difference in their world, each issue includes:

* Biblically based teaching designed just for single adults

* Columns by Mike Cavanaugh, Nancy Honeytree, other Christian leaders, and singles just like you!

* Articles on opportunities for Christian service

* Testimonies from and about single adults actively serving Christ at home and overseas

* Updates on conferences, instructional materials, audio and videotapes, and other resources designed to equip singles for service

* And more!

Why not sign up for your free subscription today?

Mike is also available to speak at your church or other Christian gathering. For further information on booking him or receiving *Single Impact,* contact:

MOBILIZED TO SERVE
7245 College Street
Lima, New York 14485
(716) 582-2790